The Field Manual For Commercial Motor Vehicle Claims

ALEX D. WEATHERBY

WEATHERBY
LAW FIRM pc

ABOUT ALEX WEATHERBY

Personal Injury Lawyer Focusing on Truck Accidents and Catastrophic Injury Claims

Alex knows first-hand what it means to suffer great loss. As a young lawyer, his own sister suffered a serious personal injury after a boating accident. In recent years, he lost another sister to leukemia. Life changes in an instant. Health issues and personal injuries are devastating. Alex uses his experience to make life better for folks after catastrophic injuries upend their lives.

He has dedicated his life to helping injured clients secure the compensation they deserve. An award-winning personal injury trial lawyer, Alex achieved a record-setting verdict in wrongful death. He actively practices truck crash law and regularly teaches other lawyers about maximizing the value of their cases. He is the owner and founding attorney of Weatherby Law Firm, PC.

Weatherby Law Firm. PC
750 Piedmont Avenue NE
Atlanta GA, 30308
alex@weatherbylawfirm.com
404-793-0026 (office)
404-793-0106 (fax)
770-363-0354 (cell)
www.weatherbylawfirm.com

Focus Areas of Practice

- **Trucking Collisions** – For over 12 years, Alex represented one of the largest trucking companies in the world. He has handled numerous trucking cases on both the plaintiff and defense sides.
- **Wrongful Death** – In 2018, Alex secured one of the top 10 wrongful death verdicts in the country. He has also recovered millions of dollars in multiple other wrongful death cases.

- **Serious Personal Injury** – Since 2011, Alex has recovered millions of dollars for clients suffering catastrophic personal injuries and has, likewise, defended major Fortune 500 companies in their personal injury cases.

Professional Leadership

Professional Organizations

- Georgia State Bar, CLE on Truck Accidents – Host (2021, 2023)
- Georgia State Bar, Professional Liability – Board Member (2019-2022)
- DeKalb County Bar Association – Member
- Georgia Trial Lawyers Association – Member

Lectures

- "Truck Accident Claims" – Sponsored by State Bar of Georgia, April 23, 2023, State Bar of Georgia
- "The Intersection of Personal Injury and Estate Law" – Sponsored by Quimbee, October 4, 2022, Online CLE
- "Truck Accident Litigation" – Sponsored by Quimbee, August 23, 2022, Online CLE
- "Dealing with the Law and Lawyers Without Stress! (Ok, Minimal Stress.)" – Sponsored by Georgia EMS Association Directors & Leadership Conference, March 29, 2022
- "Dealing with the Law and Lawyers Without Stress! (Ok, Minimal Stress.)" – Sponsored by Georgia EMS Association Annual Conference, October 11, 2021
- "Dealing with the Law and Lawyers Without Stress! (Ok, Minimal Stress.)" – Sponsored by Georgia Emergency Nurses Association Annual Conference, October 10, 2021
- "Truck Accident Claims" – Sponsored by State Bar of Georgia, August 25, 2021, State Bar of Georgia
- "A Field Manual for Truck Wreck Litigation in Georgia" – Sponsored by Lawline, May 11, 2021, Online CLE
- "A Field Manual for Truck Wrecks in Georgia" – Sponsored by MCLE, May 25, 2021, Online CLE
- "How to Litigate a Truck Accident in Georgia" – Sponsored by Quimbee, March 8, 2021, Online CLE

Publications

- "Field Manual for Commercial Motor Vehicle Law" – Fall 2023
- "Common Legal Issues in Truck Wrecks" – State Bar of Georgia, August 25, 2021
- "Preservation Issues/Expert Consults in Truck Accidents" – State Bar of Georgia, August 25, 2021
- "Common Defenses in a Legal Malpractice Case" – State Bar of Georgia, March 28, 2019

Professional Honors

- Best Truck Lawyers in Atlanta, Expertise.Com (2022)
- Super Lawyers, Rising Star (2018-2023)
- Top 20 Car Accident Verdicts in United States, TopVerdict.Com (2018)
- Top 30 Lawyers to Watch in 2018, Attorney at Law Magazine (2018)
- Top 40 Under 40 Trial Lawyers, National Trial Lawyers (2018)
- Avvo (10/10)
- William King Meadow Award, University of Georgia School of Law (2010)

Community Leadership

- Georgia State University, Lecturer, Legal Studies (2018-2019)

Education

- J.D. – University of Georgia, School of Law, Athens, GA, 2010
  - Cum Laude, Moot Court Board, Mock Trial Board, Chattahoochee Inn of Court, SBA Student Affairs
- B.A . – Samford University, Birmingham, AL, 2006
  - Summa Cum Laude

Representative Case/Client

- $27,000,000+ Verdict –Wrongful Death
- $2,250,000 Resolution – Wrongful Death of Homeless Man
- $2,000,000 Resolution – Nerve Injury
- $1,400,000 Resolution – Class Action
- $750,000 Resolution – Wrongful Death of Incarcerated Person
- $700,000 Resolution – High Speed Chase
- $550,000 Resolution – Motor Vehicle Collision

DEDICATION

This book is dedicated to my wife (Sage), my daughters (Sybil and Elyse), my parents (Al and Pam), and my sisters (Jenna, Pamela, and Ashley). Thank you for your support in my legal career. It is also dedicated to the many clients I've served over the years. Thank you for trusting me with your cases. Lastly, it is dedicated to my co-counsels. It takes a lot of trust to refer such important and impactful cases to another lawyer. Thank you for the honor and opportunity to work with you and your clients.

ACKNOWLEDGMENTS

This book would not be possible without the assistance of Jason Mance Gordon, an excellent lawyer and business professor. If you are looking for help with video or writing projects, I highly suggest contacting him! You can reach him at jmg@thebusinessprofessor.com

DISCLAIMER

Every lawyer needs a disclaimer, right? Here is ours, though I'm sure you already know it. By reading and using this book, you agree to the following disclaimer:

* <u>No Attorney-Client Relationship</u>. Neither your receipt of information from this book, nor your use of this book creates an attorney-client relationship between you and Weatherby Law Firm, PC or any of its lawyers (hereinafter, the "Firm"). You will become a client of the Firm only by execution of an engagement agreement by both you and the Firm. This engagement agreement would set forth the scope of the Firm's engagement, the fee arrangement and other relevant matters. As a matter of policy, the Firm does not accept a new client without first investigating for possible conflicts of interests and obtaining a signed engagement letter.

* <u>No Legal Advice Intended</u>. This book includes general information about legal issues and developments in the law as it pertains to commercial vehicle accidents. Such materials are for informational purposes only and may not reflect the most current legal developments. These informational materials are not intended, and must not be taken, as legal advice on any particular set of facts or circumstances. These informational materials are not all encompassing and are not intended to be applied to specific cases or circumstances, in a vacuum. The book should not be used as a substitute for competent legal advice from a licensed professional attorney in your state. You need to contact a lawyer licensed in your jurisdiction for advice on specific legal issues or problems. The book is not legal authority and is not to be cited in any legal proceeding.

* <u>No Guarantee of Results</u>. Some of the case summaries, reports of past results, and individual lawyer biographies in this book may describe past matters handled for clients of the Firm. These descriptions are meant only to provide information to the public about the activities and

experience of our lawyers. They are not intended as a guarantee that the same or similar results can be obtained in every matter undertaken by the Firm. You must not assume that a similar result can be obtained in a legal matter of interest to you. The outcome of a particular matter can depend on a variety of factors—including the specific factual and legal circumstances, the ability of opposing counsel, and, often, unexpected developments beyond the control of any client or lawyer.

* Incomplete Recitation of the Law. This book contains an overview of certain elements of commercial motor vehicle law. It is not guaranteed to be 100% accurate or complete. You must conduct your own research to verify the accuracy of the statements in this book. You may not rely on its content as a substitute for legal research.

TABLE OF CONTENTS

1

INTRODUCTION

1.1 Our Mission

The mission of every commercial motor vehicle attorney must be to make our highways safer for kids, families, and commercial motor vehicle drivers. We have two means to accomplish our mission — litigation and education. This book targets both.

As litigators, we are trained to enact change through litigation. To this end, I have built a law firm that fights for folks injured in trucking accidents and other commercial motor vehicle cases. We use highly-skilled attorneys, top-notch experts, and the justice system to make things right for injured people.

Through years of litigation, and too many trucking cases to count, I have gained a deep knowledge of the trucking industry. While I defended some of the largest insurance companies in the world, I sat in boardrooms with executives attempting to evaluate the value of life and the risk of bodily injury. Now, I sit in the living rooms of those unfortunate individuals whose families have been broken by the devastation of a tractor-trailer collision. I'm proud to profess myself in the fight for the unjustly harmed.

If litigation is our means, justice must be our end. I now work to educate other lawyers and the public about commercial motor vehicle accidents. When I was a professor, I taught students practical, real-life applications of the law. I bring that same approach to commercial vehicle training. I teach continuing legal education courses (CLEs, as they are affectionately called), training other lawyers on effective representation in commercial motor vehicle cases. And, I work to provide practical tips to the public on how their lawyer can, and should, represent them.

This book is yet another step on this road to justice. My hope is that you see me as a resource and pillar of support. I co-counsel with other lawyers on their commercial motor vehicle cases, and I represent people injured from commercial motor vehicles. If I can assist you, please contact me at 404-793-0026 or alex@weatherbylawfirm.com

1.2 Introduction

Every day, we risk our lives. Not only our lives, but the lives of those we care about most.

That's a shocking statement — I know. But, it's true.

The most dangerous thing that we do on a daily basis is to enter the highway in a motor vehicle. It is a calculated, necessary risk that we all take.

If risk is the probability of a negative outcome, then the potential gravity of that negative outcome will certainly affect our willingness to undertake that risk. I often ask myself: do we truly appreciate the nature of the risk we undertake each day?

1.3 Big Vehicles Are Scary - and They Should Be!

Based on physics (thanks, Isaac Newton), bigger vehicles are more dangerous to everyone on the highway. Big things crush little things. It is that simple. On a serious note, we know that the consequences of an automobile accident involving a large truck increases the risk of potential harm to all those involved. There are several reasons behind this:

- *Weight* - A commercial truck and trailer may weigh anywhere from 10,000 to more than 80,000 pounds. This is far more than the average civilian vehicle, which weighs between 2,500 and 6,500 pounds.[1]

- *Height* - Commercial trucks tend to sit much higher than civilian vehicles, being approximately 13.5 feet tall. This often means that, in a collision, the larger frame of the commercial vehicle will strike a civilian vehicle higher on the frame where there is less reinforcement. Civilian vehicles and their safety features are not generally designed for this type of collision.[2]

- *Materials* - The frame and other materials used in a large, commercial vehicle are heavier and stiffer than those in a smaller vehicle. In an effort to achieve efficiency, civilian vehicle manufacturers employ lighter materials. In a collision, the smaller, civilian vehicle often sustains far more damage due to its inability to absorb the force upon impact.

- *Responsiveness* - Many of the negative consequences of a vehicle crash can be mitigated by defensive driving and fast braking. The larger size and weight of the commercial vehicle mean that it is far less capable of responsiveness and taking evasive maneuvers to mitigate the effects of a vehicle crash.

---

[1] 49 C.F.R. § 390.5 (defining a commercial motor vehicle by, in part, its extreme weight).
[2] International Truck Website, https://www.internationalusedtrucks.com/semi-truck-dimensions/ (last accessed June 14, 2023).

- *Materials on Board* - Commercial vehicles often haul or carry materials that exacerbate the risks of harm in a crash. These materials may be flammable, caustic, subject to capsize, or capable of shifting in a way that causes additional harm or destruction.[3]

We undertake the risk of a catastrophic incident every time we enter the roadway. I often wonder, however, if we all under-appreciate the probability of such an occurrence.

1.4 What's Really the Likelihood of Harm?

The Federal Motor Carrier Safety Administration (the "FMCSA") is the Federal regulatory body that governs commercial motor vehicles in the United States. The FMSCA issues regulations, the Federal Motor Carrier Safety Regulations ("FMCSR"), 49 C.F.R. 300 *et seq*. The FMCSA also maintains statistics on reported wrecks with commercial motor vehicles ("CMV").

The FMCSA releases an annual report with statistics on crashes involving "large trucks" (that is, those weighing more than 10,000lbs) and buses.[4] The entire report is a necessary read for any truck accident lawyer. The noteworthy statistics, with an emphasis on the most recent year available at the time of this writing (2020), are listed below.

- In 2020, there were approximately 415,000 police-reported crashes involving large trucks.[5] 22% of those crashes were single-vehicle crashes (not including bicyclists and pedestrians).

- There were approximately 108,000 crashes *with reported injuries* involving large trucks and buses. This pertains to crashes with

---

[3] 40 C.F.R. §1037.801 (defining a "tanker truck" which is commonly used to haul flammable or toxic materials).
[4] This information is generally available on the website of the FMCSA, which as of the date of this reporting, is located here. https://www.fmcsa.dot.gov/safety/data-and-statistics/large-truck-and-bus-crash-facts (last accessed Jan. 10, 2023).
[5] Id.

injuries reported *at the scene*, as opposed to those that develop days later.[6]

- There were 4,998 large trucks and buses involved in *fatal crashes* in 2020.[7]

Standing alone, these statistics may seem arbitrary. Let's see if we can break them down a little more clearly and provide context.

The FMCSA states that there "were 13.49 fatal large truck crashes per million people in the United States in 2020."[8] This means that there was one fatal truck crash for every 71,943 persons in America.[9] I attended the University of Georgia for law school, and I am a diehard UGA fan (no offense to the other great universities out there.). Sanford Stadium has a capacity of 92,746 fans.[10] This means that one fan in that stadium, statistically, will die each year in a wreck with a large truck or bus. I don't know about you, but that brings it home for me.

While shocking when put into context, this data does not convey the immense toll of those collisions. We don't have statistics for the injuries, medical bills, property losses, and other life-changing consequences of a

---

[6] Id.
[7] Id.
[8] Id.
[9] Id.
[10] *University of Georgia, Office of University Architects for Facility Planning, https://www.architects.uga.edu/home/historic-preservation/hpmp-galleries/sanford-stadium. (last accessed Jan. 10, 2023).*

truck crash. I've sat in the room with many families, buried in medical bills and grief, who struggle to deal with the impact of a vehicle accident. The impact is overwhelming and disturbing. I cite the statistics for scope, but my intention is to bring focus on every life affected by a collision.

1.5 Why Am I Telling You All of This?

As personal injury attorneys, we are in the business of standing up for those who are hurt. Yes, we are professionals who want and need to make a living. More importantly, we stand in the ultimate position of trust when we represent clients who are in a vulnerable position. And, we must protect their interests to the best of our abilities. We developed this Manual for just that purpose. When we represent one of these affected clients, we explore every nuance that will lead to a just outcome. Hopefully, this Manual will allow you to do the same.

If you are reading this, you are likely an attorney faced with this sort of case. You may be a personal injury attorney who regularly handles non-commercial vehicle accidents. Commercial vehicle accidents, however, tend to be far more complex than those involving only civilian motorists. We talk about the specific complexities in the coming chapters. Throughout, we provide references and tips that you need to successfully navigate this challenging area of law. With this Manual, you will be armed with the best resource available to help you deliver justice.

If at any point in the process of handling one of these cases you need the assistance of a firm that focuses heavily upon truck crashes, feel free to reach out to my office – **Weatherby Law Firm, PC**, 404-793-0026, alex@weatherbylawfirm.com. We have referral and fee sharing arrangements with many other firms.

2

DO I REALLY NEED A LAWYER THAT FOCUSES ON COMMERCIAL MOTOR VEHICLE CASES? (SPOILER ALERT: YES)

Commercial vehicle attorneys have specific knowledge of the law and facts that commonly arise in truck accident cases. Also, truck accident lawyers have experience in building these cases through the collection and assembly of evidence and expert review.

The fact is: commercial motor vehicle ("CMV") cases or "Truck Cases"[11] are different than car wreck cases. The average personal injury lawyer knows the ins and outs of the Rules of the Road, causation, and damage issues. But, the standards in a CMV case are different. Unfortunately, we don't know what we don't know. This Manual will point you in the direction of what you need to learn. There are voluminous regulations that make a truck case more closely akin to a professional malpractice case than a car accident case.[12]

---

[11] At times during this book, we may use the phrase "truck case" or "truck lawyer" to refer more broadly to commercial motor vehicle cases. This is not meant to be an exclusionary term for other commercial cases. However, when writing a lengthy book, there are only so many times you can type "CMV."

[12] Castle-Foster v. Cintas Corp., 2021 US. Dist. LEXIS 28145 (S.D. Ga. Feb. 16, 2021) (permitting an expert to testify on the standards for professional drivers because it is "beyond the knowledge of a layperson.").

With a deep dive into the regulations and standards applicable to CMV drivers and motor carriers, a lawyer of reasonable ability can, of course, develop the skillset necessary to prosecute these cases. Keep in mind, there may be important pieces of evidence that are lost while you learn the standards and regulations. Some key pieces of evidence may be discarded within weeks, days, or even hours. This is true for even a well-intentioned trucking company.

Commercial vehicles are expensive assets, with the cost of new tractors nearing or exceeding $200,000.[13] The average business will have difficulty holding off-the-road an asset of that value. And, without a proper preservation letter and scene investigation, information that may be important (such as ECM-data) could be lost.[14] The FMCSR contain key provisions that limit the amount of time certain records, such as hours of service logs, must be kept.[15] These, and other issues, make quick movement by the lawyer key in a truck accident case.

2.1 Why Are Commercial Motor Vehicle Cases More Complex?

Commercial truck accidents tend to be more complicated than accidents involving civilian motorists. Throughout this book, we focus on the more procedurally complex aspects of handling a commercial vehicle case.

The following are factors that make commercial vehicle cases more complex:

- **Evidence and Investigation** – Perhaps the most demanding aspect of handling a commercial vehicle case is the intense investigation surrounding the accident. There are far more

---

[13] https://www.commercialtrucktrader.com (last accessed Jan. 11, 2023).
[14] Wiedeman v. Canal Ins. Co., 2017 U.S. Dist. LEXIS 88728 (N.D. Ga. Jun. 9, 2017).
[15] 49 C.F.R. 395.8(k).

potential causes of accidents associated with a commercial vehicle. Also, the collection of evidence often requires knowledge of all the means, methods, and places where information may be stored. It generally requires employing the services of technical, operational, and medical experts.

- **Responsible Parties** – There are more potentially responsible parties in a commercial vehicle accident than in a civilian vehicle accident. For example, responsible parties might include: the truck driver, the trucking company (and its employees), the truck or trailer manufacturer, a vehicle maintenance company, a broker/dealer, any vehicle or trailer part supplier or manufacturer, cargo manufacturer, distributor or shipper, cargo loader, intermodal equipment provider, private property owner, local, state and Federal governments, and insurance companies.[16]

- **Licenses, Standards, and Regulations** – Commercial drivers, trucking companies, and intermodal equipment providers are subject to a combination of Federal and state law, as well as industry-specific requirements or standards. Notably, you will need to be very familiar with FMCSA rules and regulations dealing with nearly every conceivable aspect of commercial motor vehicle operations.[17]

- **Employee vs Contractor Status** – Commercial vehicle accidents often involve an employer-employee or independent contractor relationship between the truck driver and trucking company. An early hurdle in this type of case is demonstrating that the driver is an actual or statutory employee of the motor carrier.[18]

---

[16] See Sec. 5.1, *supra.*
[17] See Sec. 3, *supra.*
[18] See Sec. 5.1, *supra.*

- **Insurance** – The insurance in a commercial vehicle case is significant and (at times) complex. There can be multiple policies applicable. There are also unusual responsibilities that a insurance carrier has to provide payments, despite available coverage defenses.[19]

- **Businesses** – The defendants in commercial vehicle litigation cases are generally businesses — either commercial motor carriers or insurance companies. These businesses routinely face litigation and have a great deal of experience in defending such cases. They are well versed in the regulations and how they affect operations. These realities make it more difficult to litigate against commercial motor carriers. Commercial motor carriers also tend to have more resources available to defend themselves in the event of potential legal action than individual defendants in non-commercial vehicle accidents.

- **Severity of Damages** – Because of the large size and heavy weight of the vehicles involved, commercial-vehicle accidents tend to be more serious (with regard to injuries) than small-vehicle or non-commercial accidents. Given the potential amount of damage awards, defendants necessarily invest far more resources in fighting these cases. In turn, this requires greater effort and more resources by the plaintiff or plaintiff's counsel in pursuing the case and demonstrating the extent of damage suffered.

The first step in handling a motor vehicle accident is to understand the nature of the task at hand. Being aware of these complexities will help you prepare for the undertaking.

Next, let's look at the unique role of experts in a truck case.

---

[19] See Sec. 4.1, *supra*.

2.2 Expert Issues in Truck Accidents

The cost of handling a commercial motor vehicle case, even without litigation, is generally high. One of the main reasons is the need for expert assistance at many stages of such cases. When reviewing a case, an experienced attorney will ensure that there are damages adequate to justify the expense.

When our firm signs onto a commercial motor vehicle case, we consider the need for several distinct expert types, including an accident reconstructionist, biomechanical engineer, and human factors expert. An accident reconstructionist will typically be a former police officer or an engineer specializing in reconstruction.[20] A biomechanical expert focuses on the mechanics of the interaction of the body with the force of the accident.[21] In layman's terms, they are crash dummy scientists. A human factors expert opines as to the reaction of a driver in a collision.[22]

Each of these experts is discussed further in this Manual. And, each can be critical to your case. Unfortunately, expert assistance does not come cheap. We routinely spend tens of thousands of dollars on expert advice and work product. Thus, the attorney must conduct a cost-benefit analysis at the outset.

2.3 Standards in Commercial Motor Vehicle Cases

A complex statutory scheme governs CMV cases. The corresponding regulations are a maze of Federal and state authorities.[23] There are also a

---

[20] Handley v. Werner Eters., 2022 U.S. Dist. LEXIS 47354 (M.D. Ga. 2022) (discussion of use of accident reconstructionist expert, in denying motion for summary judgment to defendant).
[21] Bowers v. Norfolk S. Corp., 537 F. Supp. 2d, 1343 (M.D. Ga. 2007) (discussion of role of biomechanic expert).
[22] Burgett v. Troy-Bilt LLC, 579 Fed. Appx. 372, 377 (6th Cir. 2014) ("Both of [biomechanical issues and human factors] are proper topics for expert testimony.").
[23] See, e.g., 49 C.F.R. Part 300 *et seq.*; O.C.G.A. § 40-1, Part 3 *et seq.*

number of publications that establish industry standards and can inform a truck lawyer's prosecution of a case.

We recommend proceeding as described below. First, review the Federal regulations in detail to determine which of the many hundreds of provisions may apply. Most of the applicable regulations are found in the Federal Motor Carrier Safety Act (FMCSR). Second, following a review of the Federal standards, review all applicable state-specific regulations to determine where the state and Federal standards may differ. Remember, the Federal regulations establish the minimum standard – state standards may be more stringent. Third, review the applicable industry guides. The Federal and state governments create guides to educate drivers. For example, the FMSCA produces a handbook on hours of service written for the benefit of drivers.[24] And, the Georgia Department of Driver's Services produces a driver's handbook.[25] These resources can be extremely helpful in understanding the factors for evaluating the standard of care and potential breaches.

2.4 Valuation in Truck Accident Cases

Truck cases often entail major damage awards. But, how do you value them?

We have evaluated dozens of commercial motor vehicle cases for some of the largest trucking companies in the United States. There are numerous factors to consider. Like any good case valuation, the starting point is always jury verdict research. Look for cases with similar fact patterns, similarly-skilled counsel, and in relevant jurisdictions.

---

[24] FMSA, Handbook for Hours of Service: https://www.fmcsa.dot.gov/sites/fmcsa.dot.gov/files/docs/Drivers%20Guide%20to%20HOS%202015_508.pdf (last accessed Jan. 11, 2023).
[25] Georgia Department of Driver's Services, Commercial Driver's Handbook, https://online.flipbuilder.com/hatf/pbsd/ (last accessed Jan. 11, 2023).

The reality of case valuation is that it is a very subjective undertaking. In most scenarios, there are a number of factors that can be pushed to sway the insurer (or ultimately a jury) as to the harm suffered and, thus, the value of a case. Identifying those facts and uncovering evidence to support them is where experienced truck-crash attorneys excel.

Another factor, not to overlook, is the experience or reputation of the opposing counsel. How the adversary (the insurance company or defense counsel) assesses your competence in mounting a successful case matters quite a lot. It may not be fair — but, it's true. If confronted with a reputable lawyer with experience and demonstrated skills in commercial motor vehicle cases, the insurance company or defense counsel likely takes a harder look at the proposed valuation. Of course, a lawyer with an unproven reputation in CMV cases can still move the needle. But, it will be more challenging. Accordingly, the lawyer and his/her skillset are noteworthy factors in valuation of cases.

Also, the reputation of the commercial driver and/or the commercial motor carrier are important factors. An insurer will view an accident involving a well-run trucking company (employing a well-trained driver) much differently than one involving a trucking company that is pushing the limits of the law.

The question becomes: how does one move the insurer (or a jury) to view the trucking company and/or the driver in their true (negligent, reckless, or unfavorable) light? There is no single answer to this question. Using the regulations, depositions, and written discovery as evidence of standards and violations thereof, an experienced commercial motor vehicle lawyer can increase the valuation substantially.

By way of example, the employment application submitted by the commercial driver often proves useful in shifting a valuation. An application, by Federal law, is certified as true and correct by the driver.[26]

---

[26] 49 C.F.R. § 391.21.

Unearthing falsehoods related to prior citations, for example, can help in moving the valuation. This is just one of many tactics discussed further in this Manual.

2.5 Partnering with a Commercial Motor Vehicle Attorney

Like most personal injury firms, we routinely co-counsel with other lawyers to handle cases. Our partners refer cases to us because we're lawyers they can trust. And, we bring the truck accident expertise necessary to properly prosecute these complex cases. Whether you partner with us or another firm, make certain that you find a partner that brings both of these qualities to the relationship. Knowledge and experience is important, but ethics are crucial.

Any attorney can refer a personal injury case to us and receive a referral fee. In accordance with the applicable law, it does not matter if you are a divorce lawyer, worker's comp. lawyer, corporate lawyer, or criminal lawyer.

Rule. 1.5(e) governs fee splits in Georgia. As it states:

> *A division of a fee between lawyers who are not in the same firm may be made only if:*
>
> 1. *the division is in proportion to the services performed by each lawyer or, by written agreement with the client, each lawyer assumes joint responsibility for the representation;*
>
> 2. *the client is advised of the share that each lawyer is to receive and does not object to the participation of all the lawyers involved; and*
>
> 3. *the total fee is reasonable.*[27]

---

[27] Ga. R. Prof. Cond. 1.5(e).

If you wish to partner with us, we make referring a case easy. Simply call (404-793-0026) or email Alex (alex@weatherbylawfirm.com). We will evaluate your case within one business day and let you know if we are able to partner with you on it.

3

OVERVIEW OF THE REGULATION OF COMMERCIAL MOTOR VEHICLES

Commercial vehicles are subject to far more regulations than non-commercial vehicles. This is true under both state and Federal law. In this section of the Manual, we introduce the regulators and regulations applicable to commercial motor-vehicle accidents.

3.1 What Is the Regulatory History of Commercial Motor Vehicle Accidents?

The Federal regulation of interstate motor carriers or trucking began primarily in 1935. In that year, Congress passed the Motor Carrier Act (MCA), which created the Interstate Commerce Commission (ICC). The ICC was charged with promulgating safety regulations to govern the industry.[28]

In 1937, the ICC began issuing regulations. These regulations have evolved over the years into what are known as the "Federal Motor Carrier Safety Regulations" (FMCSR). The FMCSR established a single body

---

[28] The Motor Carrier Act of 1935 (49 Stat. 543).

of regulations for commercial motor carriers and drivers undertaking interstate transportation. The Federal regulations are now enforced by the Federal Motor Carrier Safety Administration (FMCSA). The FMCSA was created under the Motor Carrier Safety Improvement Act of 1999 and falls under the U.S. Department of Transportation.[29]

Some states still pass their own forms of regulation in addition to these Federal provisions.[30] Because the Federal regulations create a national standard, a State cannot pass a lower standard of care and permit motor carriers to skirt by. Per 49 C.F.R. § 392.2, "[e]very commercial motor vehicle must be operated in accordance with the laws, ordinances, and regulations of the jurisdiction in which it is being operated." Likewise, 49 C.F.R. § 392.14 provides, "if a regulation of a Federal Highway Administration imposes a higher standard of care than that law, ordinance, or regulation, the Federal Highway Administration must be complied with." Thus, the regulations create minimum standards for safety.[31]

This Manual breaks down the primary FMCSRs applicable to commercial motor vehicle accidents. Even so, there are still many nuanced provisions that apply in unique and limited circumstances.

3.2 Who Regulates Commercial Motor Vehicles?

As previously mentioned, commercial motor vehicle carriers (namely, trucking companies) and commercial drivers are regulated under both Federal and state law, creating a web of regulations applicable to these entities and individuals.

---

[29] 49 U.S. Code § 113.
[30] When discussing State regulations, this Manual will focus on the Georgia regulations, as that is the location of the principal place of business of Weatherby Law Firm.
[31] 49 U.S.C. § 311.36.

3.2.1 Federal Regulation

The FMCSA is the primary body that regulates commercial motor carriers and drivers for the purpose of personal injury litigation. The FMCSA enacts the FMCSR, which can be found in 49 C.F.R. § 350 - 399. These regulations govern interstate commercial motor carriers and commercial drivers. They also cover intrastate trucking operations involving the transportation of hazardous waste.

Trucking companies are overseen by the United States Department of Transportation (DOT) and the Occupational Safety and Health Administration (OSHA), depending on the circumstances. "OSHA regulations govern the safety and health of the workers and the responsibilities of employers to ensure their safety at the warehouse, dock, construction site, and in other places truckers go to deliver and pick up loads throughout the country."[32] Most practicing personal injury lawyers will not deal with OSHA, as OSHA addresses workplace accidents. Most personal injury trial lawyers will be addressing accidents on public roads.

Accidents on public roads are overseen by the DOT. "The Department of Transportation (DOT) preempts OSHA's jurisdiction over the interstate trucking industry while traveling public road."[33] Therefore, for the vast majority of accidents, the DOT will be the organization conducting oversight, if any.

3.2.2 State Regulation

While this Manual focuses primarily on the Federal regulations, there are numerous references to state-level regulations. When referencing state-level regulations, this Manual will cite Georgia law, as this is the location of Weatherby Law Firm.

---

[32] OSHA Website, https://www.osha.gov/trucking-industry (last accessed on Jan. 11, 2023).
[33] OSHA Website, https://www.osha.gov/trucking-industry/highway-driving (last accessed on Jan. 11, 2023).

In 1972, Georgia adopted the FMCSR as the applicable safety standards for intrastate trucking activities.[34] From 1972-1984, these regulations applied to motor carriers who served the public. In 1984, the regulations were extended to include private motor carriers.

> **Pro Note:** The state of Georgia adopted the Department of Public Safety Rule book, which incorporates the standards within the Federal regulations.[35] A smart lawyer will review this book in detail.

The Georgia Public Service Commission (GPSC) is the primary state agency charged with regulating commercial motor carriers and drivers operating within the state of Georgia. More specifically, the Motor Vehicle Compliance Division, a division of the GPSC, is charged with enforcing safety regulations within the state.

> **Pro Note:** State governments are expressly preempted from regulating several very specific areas of transportation related to scheduling, routes, and fees.[36] As such, the Federal regulations and industry standards are relevant.

Remember, because the Federal regulations are <u>minimum</u> standards, State regulation can provide more stringent standards. State regulation cannot provide less stringent standards.[37]

3.2.3 Industry Standards

Commercial motor carriers also have industry standards with which they should comply. Outside of your mom-and-pop trucking companies, many larger companies produce internal training materials that create

---

[34] Ga. Comp. R. & Regs. 515-16-4-.01.
[35] Ga. Dep. of Transp. Website, https://dps.georgia.gov/georgia-department-public-safety-transportation-rulebook (last accessed Aug. 4, 2023).
[36] 49 U.S.C. § 14501 (2019).
[37] 49 C.F.R. § 392.14.

additional expectations of care. Apart from the industry standards, these training materials may contain key information particular to your incident.[38] In our practice, we've routinely discovered key information on defensive driving, cargo fastening, and more.

In addition to internal training materials, there are a number of companies that specialize in training drivers. These companies often add to the industry standards and the objective understanding of care applicable to drivers. For example, JJ Keller & Associates, Inc. ("JJ Keller") is a company that specializes in education and training for truck drivers. They have numerous handbooks that cover industry standards and best practices for truck driving.[39]

> **Pro Note:** Although training materials may be helpful in informing the standard of care, there is generally no Federal requirement for a motor carrier to train its drivers. "The Federal Motor Carrier Safety Regulations generally do not require trucking companies to train their drivers. For instance, when a driver has a valid CDL, the motor carrier may accept the CDL in lieu of subjecting the driver to a road test."[40]

This is one area where it is important to employ the services of an expert. These experienced persons may opine as to the standard of care when it is outside the knowledge of the average juror.[41]

---

[38] Glass v. Mecham, 2014 U.S. Dist. LEXIS 192653 (W.D. Okl. Jul. 7, 2014) ("Training materials for professional truck drivers are relevant to this case as evidence of what an ordinarily prudent person engaged as a professional truck driver would have done when confronted with the same circumstances.").

[39] JJ Keller's Website, https://www.jjkeller.com/ (last accessed Jan. 11, 2023).

[40] Ortiz v. Wiwi, 2012 U.S. Dist. LEXIS 137881 at *12 (M.D. Ga. 2012).

[41] Castle-Foster v. Cintas Corp., 2021 US. Dist. LEXIS 28145 (S.D. Ga. Feb. 16, 2021) (permitting an expert to testify on the standards for professional drivers because it is "beyond the knowledge of a layperson.").

3.3 What Are the Applicable Provisions of the FMCSR?

The FMCSR can be found in Title 49 of the Code of Federal Regulations (C.F.R.). These regulations can be accessed on the web at **www.fmsca.dot.gov**. Title 49 is quite extensive and it is broken into various parts. Within each of these parts are detailed subparts which contain regulations that govern the various aspects of commercial motor vehicles.

These regulations are extremely important to an attorney handling a commercial motor vehicle case. As we discuss throughout this Manual, these provisions provide the standard of care expected of the driver and commercial motor carrier, as applicable, in various situations.

It can be an important starting point for any lawyer to review the table of contents of the regulations. Once the part of the regulation(s) at issue is/are identified, you can take a deep dive into the Part in question to determine the applicable rules for your fact pattern. Here are the parts with the titles from 49 C.F.R.

PART	TITLE
Part 303	Civil Rights
Part 325	Compliance with Interstate Motor Carrier Noise Emission Standards
Part 350	Motor Carrier Safety Assistance Program (MCSAP) and High Priority Program
Part 356	Motor Carrier Routing Regulations
Part 360	Fees for Motor Carrier Registration and Insurance
Part 365	Rules Governing Applications for Operating Authority
Part 366	Designation of Process Agent
Part 367	Standards for Registration with States
Part 368	Application for a Certificate of Registration to Operate in Municipalities in the United States on the United States-Mexico International Border or Within the Commercial Zones of Such Municipalities.

PART	TITLE
Part 369	Reports of Motor Carriers
Part 370	Principles and Practices for the Investigation and Voluntary Disposition of Loss and Damage Claims and Processing Salvage
Part 371	Brokers of Property
Part 372	Exemptions, Commercial Zones, and Terminal Areas
Part 373	Receipts and Bills
Part 374	Passenger Carrier Regulations
Part 375	Transportation of Household Goods in Interstate Commerce; Consumer Protection Regulations
Part 376	Lease and Interchange of Vehicles
Part 377	Payment of Transportation Charges
Part 378	Procedures Governing the Processing, Investigation, and Disposition of Overcharge, Duplicate Payment, or Overcollection Claims
Part 379	Preservation of Records
Part 380	Special Training Requirements
Part 381	Waivers, Exemptions, and Pilot Programs
Part 382	Controlled Substances and Alcohol Use and Testing
Part 383	Commercial Driver's License Standards; Requirements and Penalties
Part 384	State Compliance with Commercial Driver's License Program
Part 385	Safety Fitness Procedures
Part 386	Rules of Practice for FMCSA Proceedings
Part 387	Minimum Levels of Financial Responsibility for Motor Carriers
Part 389	Rulemaking Procedures Federal Motor Carrier Safety Regulations
Part 390	Federal Motor Carrier Safety Regulations; General
Part 391	Qualifications of Drivers and Longer Combination Vehicle (LCV) Driver Instructors
Part 392	Driving of Commercial Motor Vehicles
Part 393	Parts and Accessories Necessary for Safe Operation

PART	TITLE
Part 395	Hours of Service of Drivers
Part 396	Inspection, Repair, and Maintenance
Part 397	Transportation of Hazardous Materials; Driving and Parking Rules
Part 398	Transportation of Migrant Workers
Part 399	Employee Safety and Health Standards

3.4 Who Is Subject to the FMCSR?

Stated broadly, the FMCSR apply to "motor carriers"[42] and "commercial vehicles."[43] As such, we begin by defining "commercial vehicles" and "motor carriers" under state and Federal law. There are specific regulations that may also come into play depending on (a) the type of vehicle, (b) the vehicle weight, (c) the interstate or intrastate travel, and (d) the material hauled.

3.4.1 What Is a "Motor Carrier"?

The "motor carrier" generally means the company that employs the drivers and places the trucks on the road. The relevant Federal rules define these terms as follows:

- The FMCSR define "*Motor Carrier*" to mean: "a **for-hire motor carrier** or **private motor carrier**. The term includes a motor carrier's agents, officers, and representatives, as well as employees responsible for hiring, supervising, training, assigning, or dispatching a driver or an employee concerned with the installation, inspection, and maintenance of motor vehicle equipment or accessories."[44]

---

[42] 49 C.F.R. § 350.105.
[43] Id.
[44] 49 C.F.R. § 350.105 (emphasis supplied).

- The FMCSR define *"For-hire motor carrier"* to mean: "a person engaged in the transportation of goods or passengers for compensation."[45]

- The FMCSR define *"Private motor carrier"* to mean "a person who provides transportation of property or passengers, by commercial motor vehicle, and is not a for-hire motor carrier.[46]

As a practical matter, these broad definitions apply to numerous companies transporting goods and persons for commerce. Therefore, we must look at additional regulations and definitions, particularly as they relate to commercial vehicles, to determine which regulations are applicable.

> **Pro Note:** The FMCSR provide exceptions from regulation under 390.3(f) to school buses, Federal/state/local government, personal property not being used for compensation, human corpses or medical transfer vehicles, non-compensated passenger vehicles between 6-15 persons, and emergency pipeline fuel vehicles. Also exempted are fire trucks and rescue vehicles, emergency vehicles, tow trucks and other vehicles providing emergency relief (49 C.F.R. § 390.23), pipeline welding trucks (49 C.F.R. § 390.38), and covered farm vehicles (49 C.F.R. § 390.39).

3.4.2 What Is a "Commercial Vehicle"?

Even if a person is not a "motor carrier" in the traditional sense (that is, they do not operate commercial vehicles for a living), they may still be subject to certain provisions of the FMCSR if they operate a commercial motor vehicle unknowingly or temporarily. A defendant that is "operating

---

[45] 49 C.F.R. § 390.5.
[46] 49 C.F.R. § 390.5T.

a commercial motor vehicle as defined in 49 C.F.R. § 390.5" is "required to comply with the FMCSR."[47]

Let's take a look at the definitions. Under 49 C.F.R. § 390.5, a *"commercial motor vehicle"* means:

> *any self-propelled or towed motor vehicle used on a highway in intrastate and interstate commerce to transport passengers or property when the vehicle:*
>
> *(A) Has a gross vehicle weight rating, gross combination weight rating, gross vehicle weight, or gross combination weight of 4,537 kg (10,001 lbs.) or more;*
>
> *(B) Is designed or used to transport more than eight passengers, including the driver, for compensation;*
>
> *(C) Is designed or used to transport more than 15 passengers, including the driver, and is not used to transport passengers for compensation; or*
>
> *(D) Is used to transport material determined to be hazardous by the secretary of the United States Department of Transportation under 49 U.S.C. § 5103 and transported in a quantity that requires placards under regulations prescribed under 49 C.F.R., Subtitle B, Chapter I, Subchapter C.[48]*

The most commonly-used definitions, in our experience, are the Gross Vehicle Weight Rating (GVWR), Gross Combination Weight Rating (GCWR), or the actual Gross Vehicle Weight (GVW) and Gross Combination Weight (GCW). Each of these is discussed further below. With the limit being only 10,001lbs, a company with a truck and trailer

---

[47] Highsmith v. Tractor Trailer Serv., 2005 U.S. Dist. LEXIS 46156 (N.D. Ga. Nov. 21, 2005).
[48] 49 C.F.R. § 390.5; O.C.G.A. § 40-1-1(8.1) (adopting the same definition for purposes of Georgia law).

may quickly jump into regulation by the FMCSR without actually realizing the implication. In instances like this, certain regulations may apply *regardless* of whether the driver has a commercial driver's license or the company is registered as a motor carrier.[49]

3.4.3 What Are Gross Vehicle Weight Ratings?

Commercial vehicles are subject to regulatory standards based largely upon their size and weight. For example, the maximum weight a truck can haul is determined by the size of the truck. Here are a few terms of art you need to understand in order to handle these claims effectively.

- *"Gross vehicle weight rating"* (GVWR) *"means the value specified by the vehicle manufacturer as the maximum design loaded weight of a single vehicle, consistent with good engineering judgment."*[50]

- *"Gross combination weight rating"* (GCWR) *"means the value specified by the vehicle manufacturer as the maximum weight of a loaded vehicle and trailer, consistent with good engineering judgment."*[51]

- *"Gross Vehicle Weight"* (GVW) *and "Gross Combination Weight"* (GCW) means the actual amount of weight from the loaded vehicle.[52]

We received a call from a colleague recently regarding a motorcycle-versus-pick-up-truck collision. The colleague advised that his client, the motorcyclist, was badly injured. However, it appeared the other side was contesting liability. When questioned, the colleague advised the pick-up truck was leaving a construction site with a trailer, hauling heavy

---

[49] Highsmith, 2005 U.S. Dist. LEXIS 46156 at *15-16 (holding that a Ford F-150, with a trailer, exceeded the GVWR of 10,001lbs subjecting the Defendants to the FMCSR).
[50] 40 C.F.R. § 1037.801.
[51] 40 C.F.R. §1037.801.
[52] Albanil v. Coast 2 Coast, Inc., 444 Fed. Appx. 788 n.11 (5th Cir. 2011).

materials. We explained the weight of the pick-up very likely subjected the defendants to the FMCSR.[53] He had no idea this may well be a significant issue in the case. These facts can be gamechangers and must be considered when evaluating a case.

> **Pro Note:** Per this broad definition, many business vehicles, such as dump trucks, delivery vans, work vans, large pickup trucks with trailers, landscaping vehicles, HVAC work vehicles, plumbing trucks and utility trucks may fall within this definition of a commercial vehicle, subjecting the defendant to the FMCSR.

3.4.4 How Do I Know if I Am Dealing with a Commercial Motor Vehicle Case?

As detailed above, it is not always obvious when a motor vehicle collision is indeed a CMV case. There can be vehicle and trailer configurations that cause a vehicle to exceed 10,000lbs and subject it to the regulations. If you are going to handle an accident involving these large, complex machines, it is important to understand the machine and the configurations in which they operate. Also, it's important to understand the lingo – especially during the discovery process. Let's review the various configurations of trucks and trailers to assist you in evaluation.

- **Bob-Tail Truck:** A tractor or truck is the large "vehicle with motive power, except a trailer, designed primarily for the transportation of property or special purpose equipment."[54] While we typically encounter tractors hauling trailers, we have handled accidents in which these tractors are riding without a trailer, commonly

---

[53] <u>Highsmith</u>, 2005 U.S. Dist. LEXIS 46156 at *15-16 (holding that a Ford F-150, with a trailer, exceeded the GVWR of 10,001lbs subjecting the Defendants to the FMCSR).
[54] 49 C.F.R. § 571.3.

referred to as "bob-tail." Standing alone, a "bobtail truck" can exceed 30,000lbs.[55]

- **Tractor-Trailer Combination:** The most classic example of a commercial motor vehicle is the tractor-trailer combination. There are numerous types; but, in general, these vehicles involve a tractor (described above) and a trailer for hauling goods. These vehicles can weigh up to 80,000lbs or more when fully loaded.[56]

- **Tanker Truck:** Tanker trucks are commercial vehicles used to transport liquids (such as fuel, chemicals, liquid waste, etc.). As the name implies, the trailer is fitted with a tank for holding liquids. Understanding this type of setup is important, as additional standards apply when a commercial motor vehicle is transporting hazardous materials.[57]

- **Flatbed Trucks:** Flatbed trucks are tractors fitted with a flat trailer used for hauling things that do not fit neatly in other types of containers. The most common configurations generally haul large machinery or parts, building materials (such as lumber or steel beams), manufactured homes, vehicles, etc. The defining characteristic is that the flatbed truck or trailer does not have walls or sides. Cargo is generally strapped to the flatbed to secure it.

- **Logging Truck:** Logging trucks are very similar to flatbed trucks, but they have a unique trailer configuration developed specifically to haul large timbers. The trailer lacks a flat bed. The trailer is designed similarly to the letter holders that are commonly used in offices. The logs are stacked within upright forks that protrude from the frame of the trailer. These trailers are particularly dangerous because they go into remote places to load; they take a

---

[55] https://myautomachine.com/how-much-does-a-bobtail-truck-weigh/ (last accessed Jan. 13, 2023).

[56] https://www.onsitetruckaz.com/post/how-much-does-a-semi-truck-weigh-ultimate-guide-2022 (last accessed Feb. 2, 2023).

[57] 40 C.F.R. §1037.801.

beating; and they pull a very unevenly-distributed load. Also, the cargo (logs) tends to extend far behind the back of the trailer in un-even lengths.

> **Pro Note:** Intrastate logging trucks operating in Georgia are subject to the Georgia Forest Product Trucking Rules. These standards vary somewhat from those applicable to traditional commercial motor carriers. Coverage of these specific regulations is outside the scope of this Manual; but, please contact us if you have specific questions or need help with this type of case.

- **Box Trucks (Straight Trucks):** A box truck is simply a heavy-duty vehicle equipped with an enclosed container that is affixed to the rear frame of the vehicle. Good examples to think of are U-Haul and Midas vehicles. Unlike a big rig, the box truck does not employ a separate trailer to transport goods. These vehicles are routinely used by businesses to deliver goods over short distances. Many commercial motor carriers incorporate this type of vehicle into its service model. This is particularly true because certain box trucks (under 26,001lbs GVWR) do not require a CDL to operate.[58]

- **Pick-Up Trucks:** Somewhat surprisingly to an unfamiliar lawyer, a pick-up truck with a trailer can be a CMV. When the pick-up truck and trailer exceeds 10,000lbs, it is subject to certain FMCSR.[59] These smaller truck-trailer combinations are often referred to as "hot shots".

---

[58] FMCSA, Exemptions to the Federal Motor Carrier Safety Regulations https://www.fmcsa.dot.gov/registration/commercial-drivers-license/driver-combination-vehicle-gcwr-less-26001-pounds-required (last accessed Mar. 1, 2023).
[59] Highsmith, 2005 U.S. Dist. LEXIS 46156 at *15-16 (holding that a Ford F-150, with a trailer, exceeded the GVWR of 10,001lbs subjecting the defendants to the FMCSR).

● **Cement Trucks:** Cement trucks, also known as concrete mixers, are used to mix and haul cement in a ready-to-pour state.[60] These vehicles have all sorts of modifications to allow the mounting of a large motorized drum to the frame of the vehicle. Cement trucks are at risk of many of the accidents common to large commercial trucks. However, the unique risk associated with cement trucks includes tipping over. The weight of these trucks (26,001 - 40,000 lbs.) combined with the manner the cement is stored on the vehicle makes it more susceptible to overturn.

Cement trucks also implicate multiple potentially liable individuals in the event of an accident, as these trucks are used in carrying out larger projects. Some potentially liable parties might include the driver, cement company, shipping company, sub-contractor, general construction contractor, truck, part, or specialty manufacturer, and local or state governments.[61]

● **Dump Truck:** Dump trucks come in many forms and sizes. The premise behind the vehicle is that the bed of the vehicle is equipped with hydraulics that allow one end to rise into the air. The contents of the truck are then expelled by gravity from the other end. Dump trucks are a form of vocational truck used to haul garbage, demolition, or granular materials, such as sand or grains. It generally has a boxed rear (bed) with an open or soft-covered top.

Dump trucks are very common in Georgia as a result of the large amount of farming and agriculture in the state. Accidents involving these vehicles give rise to unique risks and potentially liable parties.[62] It is common for cargo or debris to fall from

---

[60] 40 C.F.R. § 1037.801.

[61] National Ready Mix Concrete Association, Statistical Compilation, https://www.concreteinfocus-digital.com/nrcq/summer2018/MobilePagedArticle.action?articleId=1395575&#articleId1395575 (last accessed Jun. 1, 2023).

[62] Engineering News Record, Statistical Compilation, https://www.enr.com/articles/46126-serious-dump-and-read-mix-delivery-truck-accidents-edge-higher (last accessed Jun. 15, 2023).

these trucks when not properly loaded. Also, dump trucks are frequently used as a part of larger projects. Potentially-liable parties include the driver, shipping company, cargo owner (e.g., farmer), vehicle manufacturer or specialty parts manufacturer, and state or local governments.

- **Garbage Trucks:** Garbage trucks are present in every municipality and county in Georgia. These are specialty trucks constructed with any number of configurations to allow for the collection and transport of garbage. Common forms of garbage truck include side loaders, front loaders, grapple trucks, pneumatic collection, and rear loaders (the most common). All of these configurations entail heavy frames and motorized systems (such as hydraulics).

  The large, bulky nature of the vehicle combined with the excessive weight makes it very difficult to handle and maneuver on the open road. Also, the vehicles generally operate in open traffic and make routine stops. Sanitation engineers routinely ride on the side of the vehicle and step on and off to collect refuse. Operators employ the mechanical collection arms without good visibility of the rear and sides of the vehicle. Civilians are often walking on the sidewalks or roadways where these vehicles are operating. This operational pattern dramatically increases the likelihood of collisions with other vehicles and injuries.[63]

  Garbage trucks give rise to potential liability among numerous parties including drivers, sanitation engineers, vehicle manufacturers, specialty parts manufacturers, waste management companies, and local or state governments.

- **Tow Trucks:** Tow trucks, often called wreckers, are specialty forms of commercial vehicle used to transport vehicles. They

[63] Solid Waste Association of North America noted a "unprecedented uptick in fatalities" in 2019. https://www.recyclingtoday.com/news/waste-industry-fatalities-swana/ (last accessed Jun. 15, 2023).

come in two common configurations: 1) a long, flat-bed truck that has a hydraulic function to tip the bed and allow for loading of one or more vehicles, and 2) a truck with a mounted hydraulic/mechanical system for winching up one end of a vehicle and transporting it in a suspended state.[64]

The flatbed model of tow truck gives rise to risks of tipping over and loss of cargo. Also, the load sits very high on the bed of the vehicle, which makes handling and maneuvering the vehicle more difficult. The winching-lift configuration creates a unique handling situation for inexperienced drivers. Also, it gives rise to the possibility of mechanical malfunction and the vehicle working loose from the wench.

Numerous potentially liable individuals may be implicated in a tow-truck accident, including the driver, tow company, vehicle manufacturer of specialty part manufacturer, and cargo loader.

> **Pro Note:** The various truck configurations discussed herein may also be statutorily defined. It is important to review the local definitions to see if the vehicle in question is subject to unique regulations.

* **Buses:** Buses have their own special Federal regulations; though, many of the standards laid out in the FMCSR can be applied to bus operations. Under Federal law, "bus" means a motor vehicle with motive power, except a trailer, designed for carrying **more than 10 persons**.[65] Georgia law, likewise, defines "bus" to mean "every motor vehicle designed for carrying **more than ten passengers** and used for the transportation of persons and every motor vehicle, other than a taxicab, designed and used for the

---

[64] Lemon Bin Vehicle Guides, Types of Tow Trucks, https://lemonbin.com/types-of-tow-trucks/ (last accessed Jun. 15, 2023).
[65] 49 C.F.R. 571.3.

transportation of persons for compensation."[66] Specialty types of bus defined under the Federal regulations include: *"School bus"*; *"Multifunction school activity bus* (MFSAB)"; and, *"Multipurpose passenger vehicle."*[67] Buses are subject to very specific regulations with regard to design and operations.[68]

Depending on the owner, use, and function of the business, buses implicate a number of potentially liable individuals in the event of an accident. These include the bus driver, bus owner, management company, business contracting bus services, vehicle or specialty parts manufacturer, and state or local governments.

• **Passenger-Carrying Vehicles (over 8 Persons):** A passenger carrying van for over 8 persons is subject to certain regulation by the FMCSA.

"Motor carriers operating 9 to 15 passenger-carrying commercial motor vehicles for direct compensation, regardless of the distance traveled, are subject to the safety standards in part 385 and parts 390 through 396 [of the Federal Motor Carrier Safety Regulations]."[69] The FMCSR require that the operator register with the FMCSA and place its USDOT number and business name on the vehicle. There are other requirements too, including maintaining an accident register, meeting driver qualification and medical exam requirements, complying with hours of service regulations, and more.[70]

Likewise, motor carriers "operating 9 to 15 passenger-carrying commercial motor vehicles for indirect compensation, regardless of the distance traveled, are required to: (1) Register with FMCSA; (2) Mark their commercial motor vehicles with the USDOT

---

[66] O.C.G.A. 40-1-1(7).
[67] 49 C.F.R. § 571.3.
[68] 49 C.F.R. § 392.62.
[69] https://www.fmcsa.dot.gov/registration/small-passenger-carrying-vehicles (last accessed Feb. 2, 2023).
[70] Id.

identification number; (3) Maintain an accident register; (4) Comply with the prohibition against drivers texting while driving; and, (5) Comply with the cellular phone restrictions for drivers."[71]

These examples are not meant to be exhaustive. Instead, they are meant to show the diversity of commercial vehicles subject to Federal regulation. As you have likely determined, the vehicles subject to the Federal regulations are far broader than one might initially assume. Collisions involving each of these types of vehicle implicate a broad range of Federal and state rules.

3.4.5 Is the Defendant an Interstate or Intrastate Motor Carrier?

The state or Federal agencies that regulate a "commercial motor vehicle" or "motor carrier" depend upon whether the carrier is classified as an interstate carrier or intrastate carrier.[72] This is important as state regulations may vary from the Federal regulation. For example, to drive interstate a person must be 21 years of age, while intrastate drivers need be only 18 years of age (in the State of Georgia).[73]

In its most basic form, an "intrastate carrier" means a vehicle "used on a highway in intrastate commerce to transport passengers or property" and is (a) 10,001lbs or more, (b) designed to carry more than 10 passengers, or (c) transports hazardous materials.[74] However, determining what is used for "intrastate commerce" or "interstate commerce" can be a challenge. For example, if a shipment remains totally within 1 state, the load may still be considered as involving interstate commerce. The FMCSA has provided this guidance:

---

[71] Id.
[72] 49 C.F.R. § 390.3.
[73] 49 C.F.R. § 383.71.
[74] O.C.G.A. § 40-2-1(5) (2020).

> *Interstate commerce is determined by the essential character of the movement, manifested by the shipper's fixed and persistent intent at the time of shipment, and is ascertained from all of the facts and circumstances surrounding the transportation. When the intent of the transportation being performed is interstate in nature, even when the route is within the boundaries of a single State, the driver and CMV are subject to the FMCSRs.*[75]

The distinction, however, is somewhat less important in Georgia, because Georgia has adopted nearly all of the FMCSRs as the standard for intrastate trucking on public roads.[76]

Because a transportation may be interstate in nature, even if the actual route is wholly in-state, the question becomes, "what is the intended ultimate destination of the goods being transported?" As a simple rule, if the ultimate destination of the shipment is out of state, the transportation is likely interstate in nature.

The important takeaway is that determining whether a transportation is interstate or strictly intrastate in nature is not straightforward.

3.4.6 Exemptions from the FMCSR

Not every commercial vehicle is subject to regulation under the FMCSR. While Georgia has adopted the Federal regulations, a Federal statute specifically exempts certain types of vehicle.[77]

In the paragraph below, we have summarized and shortened the statute for ease of reading and understanding. This will assist you in obtaining a general idea as to the excepted vehicles. Our recommendation is to read each line of the statute. You will see that

---

[75] FMCSA-RG-390.3T-Q006 (Eff. April 4, 1997).
[76] Ga. Comp. R. & Regs. R. 570-38-1-.05 (2020).
[77] 49 USC § 13506.

there are exceptions for certain types of motor vehicles and certain types of transportation.

Per 49 USC § 13506, the following are specific categories to which the FMCSR does not apply:

> *(a) Neither the Secretary nor the Board has jurisdiction under this part over:*
>
> > *(1) a motor vehicle transporting only school children and teachers to or from school;*
> >
> > *(2) a motor vehicle providing taxicab service;*
> >
> > *(3) a motor vehicle owned or operated by or for a hotel and only transporting hotel patrons between the hotel and the local station of a carrier;*
> >
> > *(4) a motor vehicle controlled and operated by a farmer and transporting the farmer's agricultural or horticultural commodities and products; or supplies to the farm of the farmer [with various exceptions for specific products][78];*
> >
> > *(5) a motor vehicle controlled and operated by a cooperative association or by a federation of cooperative associations… [that doesn't engage in interstate transportation and including various exemptions]*
> >
> > *(6) transportation by motor vehicle of ordinary livestock; agricultural or horticultural commodities [various exceptions], other exempt commodities, cooked or uncooked fish [non-canned/preserved]; and livestock and poultry feed and agricultural seeds and plants [various exceptions];*

---

[78] For sake of brevity, the items in brackets [] have been supplied by the author to save time in reading. In addition, the author has summarized portions of the statute to provide the reader with a general understanding of the statute, as opposed to a direct quotation.

(7) a motor vehicle used only to distribute newspapers;

(8) vehicles used to transport individuals or baggage incident to air travel,

(9) the operation of a motor vehicle in a national park or national monument

(10) a motor vehicle carrying not more than 15 individuals in a single, daily roundtrip to commute to and from work;

(11) vehicles transporting pallets, containers, or other shipping devices;

(12) transportation of natural, crushed, vesicular rock to be used for decorative purposes;

(13) transportation of wood chips;

(14) brokers for motor carriers of passengers, except as provided in section 13904(d) - provisions concerning registration of brokers.

(15) transportation of broken, crushed, or powdered glass; or

(16) the transportation of passengers by 9 to 15 passenger motor vehicles operated by youth or family camps that provide recreational or educational activities.

(b) Except to the extent the Secretary or Board, as applicable, finds it necessary to exercise jurisdiction to carry out the transportation policy of section 13101, neither the Secretary nor the Board has jurisdiction under this part over:

(1) transportation provided entirely in a municipality, in contiguous municipalities.... [under specific circumstance]).

(2) transportation by motor vehicle provided casually, occasionally, or reciprocally but not as a regular occupation or business.... [with various exception and qualification under 49 C.F.R. § 372.101];

(3) the emergency towing of an accidentally wrecked or disabled motor vehicle;

(4) transportation by a motor vehicle designed or used to transport not fewer than 9, and not more than 15, passengers (including the driver) .... [under specific circumstances].

An additional consideration is that commercial driver's license (CDL) standards and Georgia Rules of the Road apply to the situation, even if the FMCSR do not. There are exceptions to the exceptions too, so pay particular attention to the unique circumstances of your case.

3.5 Types of Commercial Vehicle Accidents

Commercial motor vehicle accidents can occur in a variety of manners. Common accident scenarios involving commercial vehicles can be grouped into three broad categories:

* Single-Vehicle Accidents,

* Vehicle-Pedestrian Accidents, and

* Two (or more) Vehicle Collisions

In our firm, we focus on bodily injury claims resulting from accidents with commercial motor vehicles. As such, we limit the coverage in this Manual to the latter scenarios. We have handled over 60 truck accident cases, including numerous ones in each of these categories.

3.5.1 Common Impacts with any Type of Commercial Vehicle

Common scenarios involving civilian passenger and commercial vehicle collisions include the following:

* **Direct (Head-On) Collision** – This normally takes place when one vehicle veers into the on-coming lane. It also arises when a vehicle accidentally enters a one-way street or lane.

* **T-Bone** – A T-bone collision most commonly occurs when one vehicle runs a stop sign or red light; when a vehicle is backing out into a street; or when a vehicle pulls out in front of on-coming traffic to cross an intersection or to make a turn.

* **Rear End** – A rear end collision is perhaps the most common type. This occurs most frequently when a vehicle is following too closely.

* **Back-Up Collision** – A back-up collision is when one vehicle cannot see the person or property to the rear of the vehicle and backs into it. The most tragic of these cases occur when children are playing in the street and a driver fails to adequately inspect the area or has limited vision behind the vehicle.

* **Stopped Vehicles** – Commercial trucks often break down or have to stop on the side or middle of the roadway (such as trucks offloading deliveries). This often results in an accident when unaware motorists fail to recognize the stopped vehicle and crash into it or into other vehicles in an attempt to avoid the stopped vehicle. (The commercial driver may be to blame when, for example, they fail to place warning markers behind the vehicle).

* **Improper Maneuvers** – The term improper maneuver is a very broad descriptor for when a truck driver fails to follow the Rules of the Road. There are many, many scenarios that constitute a improper maneuver. Some common examples include:

- ○ **Lane Change** – Improper changing of lanes and/or merging into another vehicle.

- ○ **Narrow Turn** – The commercial vehicle turns too sharply and contacts a stationary vehicle.

- ○ **Wide Turn** – The rules under which large commercial trucks operate, including the CDL Manual and FMCSR, set forth specific rules about how large trucks should complete turns without putting other drivers at risk.

- ○ **Left Turn** – Left turns require a driver to cross a lane of traffic to enter the road. Accidents can occur with traffic coming from either direction. Also, the time it takes to complete the turn is longer, thus exposing the driver to increased risk of collision with fast-moving vehicles.

The above-referenced accidents are common across all commercial vehicles. Next, let's take a look at some types of accident common to big rigs.

3.5.2 Common Impacts with Tractor-Trailers

The types of accidents that we want to address with greater specificity in this Manual are accidents involving tractor-trailers. At first glance, it may seem that this type of vehicle accident is easy to understand or straightforward. It is worth noting that there are various collisions or accidents that are unique to trucks and trailer combinations. Some common forms of truck and trailer accidents include:

- * **Jack Knife** – A jack knife happens when the trailer swings out wide to form a near 90-degree angle with the truck that is pulling it. It often happens as a result of hard braking (fast stop) by the truck or when the brakes on the trailer are not properly engaging. It may also be caused by the weight of the trailer making the wheels of the trailer lose traction, pushing the tractor or trailer sideways. Fast stops from high rates of speed, braking while going down steep hills, and hard braking on slippery roads are some other common scenarios resulting in jack knives. In any situation, the trailer (rather than staying in line with the truck) either swings outside of the truck or pushes the truck sideways.

• **Underride** – Large commercial trailers often sit high on the trailer's chassis (above the height of the wheels) to allow for maximum, flat hauling surface on the trailer. An underride is when a smaller vehicle crashes into the trailer and that vehicle goes underneath the trailer chassis. Regulations require underride guards on trailers just for this reason. This type of crash is typically catastrophic, as occupants of passenger vehicles are particularly vulnerable in such an accident. An underride may occur from the side (while turning) or rear of the vehicle.

We handled a particularly catastrophic underride case involving a high-speed police chase. The result was a civilian vehicle that went fully underneath the trailer, removing the roof section. Two persons were killed, and three children were seriously injured. After no pre-suit offer from the defendants, we filed suit and ultimately negotiated a full policy limits resolution for our client.

- **Overturn or Rollover** – Any vehicle is susceptible to overturn or rollover. Vehicles that sit higher on the frame, especially those with narrow wheel bases, are more likely to overturn in an accident. Trucks pulling a trailer carry high rollover risk, as the weight of the trailer can overturn the truck. The risk of rollover increases with the weight of goods on the trailer, the height at which the goods are loaded, tire blowouts, load shifting, and the speed of travel or turning.

> **Pro Note:** An overturn or rollover case may be paired with another type of case, such as falling cargo. In such a situation, a number of potential regulations may be implicated, which makes paying particular attention to the rules essential.

- **Falling Cargo** – Falling cargo occurs when poorly-secured items fall from a vehicle or trailer. Liability results when the cargo hits other vehicles or pedestrians, or creates a roadway hazard that causes a subsequent collision. Cargo falls may be an issue for flat, open-bed, or open-top trailers. These configurations are common for vehicles hauling building materials, industrial parts, machinery, vehicles, etc. The cargo may be improperly loaded or not secured appropriately. Cargo that is loaded at the beginning of a trip may shift to become insecure during travel, such as when the driver hits large bumps or takes sharp turns. As such, failure to stop and conduct load inspections becomes relevant. Also, falling cargo issues arise in conjunction with other forms of trailer-related accident (such as the jack knife). For this reason, the Federal Motor Carrier Safety Regulations and Georgia law require drivers to inspect their loads at various points in the transportation process. [79]

Our point in describing these various types of vehicle accidents is to make you aware of how diverse CMV accidents can be. Some collisions

---

[79] 49 C.F.R. § 392; O.C.G.A. § 40-6-248.

may involve two or more of the above-referenced types of collision. For example, a truck that jack knifes in the road may sideswipe some vehicles and rear-end another — all while the trailer swings wide into an on-coming lane and causes a head-on collision. As you can tell, the potential for tragic scenarios in a large-vehicle collision is extremely broad.

At our firm, we have handled numerous different types of commercial motor vehicle accidents. In a recent case, we represented a young doctor who was traveling caravan-style with her mother to visit a home for sale. It was a sunny, bright day. The daughter was following closely behind the mother's car when a truck hauling steel careened into the back of her, causing severe injuries. The photographs of the accident demonstrated that she was inches from losing her life. After reconstructing the accident, we determined the driver for the steel hauler had been distracted or asleep.

Now, let's move on to some standards and responsibilities of motor carriers and drivers that are meant to keep us all safe on the highway.

4

WHAT ARE THE MOTOR CARRIER'S RESPONSIBILITIES?

An early step in working a commercial-motor-vehicle-collision case is to determine whether there have been any violations of either the rules of the road and/or the Federal and state standards applicable to the driver and the commercial carrier.

Throughout this portion of the Manual, we are going to discuss the broad array of standards applicable to motor carriers in interstate (and sometimes intrastate) transportations. As previously discussed, the Federal Motor Carrier Safety Regulations (FCMSR) were adopted, almost entirely, as the minimum safety standards for intrastate motor carriers in Georgia.[80] However, understanding the need for state-level autonomy, the FCMSR specifically allow states and local municipalities to create and enforce *more restrictive* rules and regulations than FMCSA.[81]

---

[80] Ga. Comp. R. & Regs. R. 515-16-4-.01.
[81] 49 C.F.R. § 390.9.

> **Pro Note:** Georgia's Commercial Driver's Manual lays out the standards for achieving CDL licensure in Georgia. Thus, these requirements have become standards of operation within the state.[82]

The requirements of the FMCSR can be found in 49 C.F.R. §, Chapter B, 350 – 399. The specific Georgia rules can be found within the Transportation Rules of Georgia Department of Public Safety.[83] Because Georgia has adopted the FMCSR, we can focus on the FMCSRs when reviewing the standards for interstate and intrastate commercial motor carriers and drivers.

While this handbook cannot cover all of the responsibilities of a motor carrier in a particular situation, we will discuss those more commonly seen.

- **Duty to Investigate:** As detailed below, prior to engaging the driver for employment, a motor carrier is required to investigate truck drivers. This includes (a) a pre-employment drug screen,[84] (b) confirmation of physical fitness,[85] (c) inquiries with DOT regulated employers,[86] (d) a written application certified as true,[87] and (e) a road test or confirmation of valid CDL licensure.[88] A motor carrier's failure to complete its investigation may be the basis for a separate claim for negligent hiring.

- **Duty to Maintain:** The Federal Regulations require a trucking company to inspect, repair, and maintain its vehicles (truck,

---

[82] Georgia Department of Driver's Services, Commercial Driver's Handbook, https://online.flipbuilder.com/hatf/pbsd/ (last accessed Jan. 11, 2023).

[83] Georgia Dep't of Pub. Safety, https://dps.georgia.gov/sites/dps.georgia.gov/files/imported/vgn/images/portal/cit_1210/6/32/52465205Chapter_1_DPS_Transportation_Rules.pdf (last accessed Feb. 6, 2023).

[84] 49 C.F.R. § 382.301.

[85] 49 C.F.R. § 391.43.

[86] 49 C.F.R. § 391.23.

[87] 49 C.F.R. § 391.21.

[88] 49 C.F.R. § 383.23; 49 C.F.R. 383.133.

trailer, etc.) and equipment in good working order. This includes performing a detailed, yearly inspection. The company must maintain repair records for a minimum of 18 months.[89]

- **Duty to Instruct:** Trucking companies are required to be familiar with trucking regulations.[90] Drivers are likewise required to be "instructed regarding, and shall comply with," the applicable regulations.[91] This does not mean, however, that Federal law requires the trucking company to train their drivers. "The Federal Motor Carrier Safety Regulations generally do not require trucking companies to train their drivers."[92] Nevertheless, trucking companies often provide training. When such training is offered, the company's own training materials can be relevant in establishing a standard of care.

- **Duty to Supervise:** The carrier has a duty to supervise the conduct of a driver for compliance with the driving standards. "Whenever . . . a duty is prescribed for a driver or a prohibition is imposed upon the driver, it shall be the duty of the motor carrier to require observance of such duty or prohibition."[93]

- **Duty to Not Encourage, Coerce, or Facilitate a Violation:** The duty to supervise further imposes a duty on the carrier to not act in concert with the driver to disregard established standards. Per the regulation, "[n]o person shall aid, abet, encourage, or require a motor carrier or its employees to violate the rules of this chapter."[94] Further, motor carriers may not harass drivers to break the rules.[95]

---

[89] 49 C.F.R. § 396.
[90] 49 C.F.R. § 390.3.
[91] Id.
[92] Ortiz v. Wiwi, 2012 U.S. Dist. LEXIS 137881 at *12 (M.D. Ga. 2012).
[93] 49 C.F.R. § 390.11.
[94] 49 C.F.R. § 390.13.
[95] 49 C.F.R. § 390.36.

- **Compliance and Facilitation:** If a possible or potential violation of standards gives rise to a collision or accident, the motor carrier has an affirmative obligation to comply with a resulting regulatory investigation by the FMCSA concerning driver safety and potential violations of the rules.[96] As part of this compliance obligation, the motor carrier must specifically maintain and store certain documents related to compliance at the carrier's central place of business.[97] These documents are often not discoverable in litigation, due to a Federal privilege.[98]

- **Non-Delegation of Duties:** A commercial motor carrier may not avoid certain responsibilities by outsourcing duties to a third-party. In one case, for example, a motor carrier attempted to avoid liability for failure to maintain a rusted drag link, which ultimately caused a collision. The motor carrier argued it could not be liable for negligent maintenance because it outsourced all maintenance to a third-party. The court held that this outsourcing did not insulate the motor carrier from liability, stating "[a] reasonable jury could conclude that [the motor carrier] had a duty under the FMCSR to properly maintain and inspect the tractor/truck and that they have failed to do so."[99]

This is only an overview of some of the commonly litigated responsibilities of a motor carrier. There are additional less-common, but equally relevant standards. And, even the standards cited above may have exceptions.

The following sections discuss many of the detailed requirements on motor carriers to remain in compliance with the FMCSR.

---

[96] 49 C.F.R. § 390.15.
[97] 49 C.F.R. § 390.15; 49 C.F.R. § 390.29.
[98] 49 U.S.C. § 504(f).
[99] Esteras v. TRW, Inc., 2006 U.S. Dist. LEXIS 60437, No. 3:CV-03-1906 (M.D. Pa., Aug. 25, 2006).

4.1 What Are the Registration Requirements for a Motor Carrier?

If you decide to tackle an accident case involving a commercial vehicle, one of your initial actions should be to obtain all relevant information available about the motor carrier undertaking the transportation.

We dedicate a section of this handbook to the types of discovery requests you may serve in litigation. Here, we want to make certain you have a basic understanding of the types of available information concerning the motor carrier.

Interstate motor carriers are required to register with the FMCSA to acquire operating authority within a given area and to obtain any hazardous-material permit.[100] Interested persons can obtain a copy of the application for a motor carrier through the FMCSA.[101]

Before making a blanket request for the commercial carrier's registration information, you may want to familiarize yourself with the registration requirements applicable to the motor carrier (and others involved in the transportation process). Specifically, you should focus on 49 USC § 13901 - 13909 (and the accompanying regulations) which specify the following:

* §13901. Requirements for registration.

* §13902. Registration of motor carriers.

* §13903. Registration of freight forwarders.

* §13904. Registration of brokers.

* §13905. Effective periods of registration.

---

[100] 49 USC § 139.
[101] 49 C.F.R. § 365.117.

- §13906. Security of motor carriers, motor private carriers, brokers, and freight forwarders.

- §13907. Household goods agents.

- §13908. Registration and other reforms.

- §13909. Availability of information.[102]

Notably, 49 C.F.R. § 390.201 identifies "who must register with FMCSA under the Unified Registration System ["URS"], the filing schedule, and general information pertaining to persons subject to the Unified Registration System, registration requirements."[103] The FMCSA is currently revising this rule and has implemented temporary procedural requirements for filing. Therefore, while it is clear that filing must take place, the format and timing of the filings are subject to change.[104]

Generally, pursuant to the applicable code sections, motor carriers must file a Form MCSA-1 (which is the URS application) online with the FMCSA. The carrier must make this filing every 24 months. The MCSA-1 identifies the operations with FMCSA oversight, requests operating authority (as applicable), and requests hazardous-materials safety permits (as applicable).[105] Failure to do so may subject the motor carrier to penalties.[106] The regulation contains numerous definitions and detailed explanations. Therefore, please do not accept this summary as a complete guide. We encourage you to read the regulation in detail.

The URS application process begins with acquiring a USDOT number.[107] Not only is the assignment of a USDOT number part of the registration process, each carrier must make certain any vehicle

---

[102] 49 USC § 13901 - 13909.
[103] 49 C.F.R. § 390.201 (items in brackets supplied).
[104] 82 F.R. 5292 (2017).
[105] 49 C.F.R. § 390.201.
[106] 49 C.F.R. § 390.201.
[107] 49 C.F.R. § 390.201(c)(iii)(2).

undertaking transportation is marked with the name of the motor carrier and the USDOT number.[108] This number will be key in your search to uncover the relevant facts concerning the motor carrier.

Before the FMCSA will issue or activate a USDOT Number, the carrier must provide proof of "financial responsibility" within 90 days.[109] The carrier must also have insurance or be bonded adequately to meet the Federal requirement.[110]

Once the registration requirements are met, the carrier may begin operations.[111]

4.2 What Is the Uniform Carrier Registration System (UCRS)?

The FMCSA created the Uniform Carrier Registration System (UCRS) as a single-state registration system for interstate carriers. This simplified the registration process by eliminating the requirement to register in each state of operations.[112]

> **Pro Note:** For motor carriers operating purely intrastate, there may be state-specific registration requirements. For example, Georgia requires intrastate carriers to register with its Georgia Intrastate Motor Carrier Registration program.[113]

The registrant chooses a "base state" for registration - usually the primary state of doing business.[114] For purposes of collecting potentially relevant information on the motor carrier, this simplifies the process for

---

[108] 49 C.F.R. § 390.21.
[109] 49 C.F.R. § 390.205(a).
[110] 49 C.F.R. § 387.
[111] 49 C.F.R. § 390.201; 49 C.F.R. § 385.301.
[112] 49 USC § 14504a(f).
[113] GA Dep't of Pub. Safety Website, https://gamccd.net/UCR/UCRGa.aspx (last accessed Feb. 8, 2023).
[114] 49 USC § 14504a(a)(2).

the trial lawyer in acquiring the motor carrier's registration application and information.

4.3 Establishing a Registered Agent

Motor Carriers are required to designate and list process agents in each state "in which it is authorized to operate and for each state traversed during such operations."[115] Brokers are required to designate a registered agent in each state "in which its offices are located or in which contracts will be written."[116] Freight forwarders are, likewise, required to designate a registered agent in each state "in which its offices are located or in which contracts will be written."[117] While you will check the Secretary of State's office to identify the registered agent for service of process and information requests, it may be helpful to compare the state-listed registered agent with the registered agent identified pursuant to the FMCSR.

4.4 Insurance

The FMCSR require that any motor carrier must file proof of liability insurance prior to operating.[118] As it states for passenger-carrying vehicles, "[n]o motor carrier shall operate a motor vehicle transporting passengers until the motor carrier has obtained and has in effect the minimum levels of financial responsibility as set forth in § 387.33 of this subpart."[119] And, as it states for property carrying commercial vehicles, "a person that registers to conduct operations in interstate commerce as a for-hire motor carrier, a broker, or a freight forwarder must file evidence of financial responsibility as required under part 387, subparts C and D of this subchapter."[120]

---

[115] 49 C.F.R. § 366.4(a).
[116] 49 C.F.R. § 366.4(b).
[117] 49 C.F.R. § 366.4(c).
[118] 49 C.F.R. § 387.31; 49 C.F.R. § 390.205.
[119] 49 C.F.R. § 387.31.
[120] 49 C.F.R. § 390.205.

The minimum limits of "financial responsibility" depend on the type of activity performed. For example, for passenger-carrying vehicles, the minimum limits of financial responsibility are $1,500,000 (15 or more passenger vehicles) and $5,000,000 (16 or more passenger vehicles).[121] There are too many iterations to list here. Therefore, we recommend that you review 49 C.F.R. § 387 Parts C and D.

It is common for a motor carrier to have more than one insurance provider. Obtaining these records from the FMCSA may provide valuable early information in the settlement and negotiation process.

4.5 What Are the Georgia Registration Requirements?

As noted above, the UCRS obviated the need to register in multiple states. The UCRS, however, requires the designation of a base state.[122]

Once you identify the base state, in our experience, you will find the majority of the state-specific registration information. That is not to say, however, that a carrier cannot register in multiple states. And, there are scenarios in which this makes sense for the carrier. So, you should use any information surrounding the carrier - names, USDOT numbers, agents, insurance policies, etc. - to determine all states of registration. This can be particularly important if the carrier has a subsidiary operating units registered in different states.

In Georgia, an intrastate carrier must meet the registration requirements under O.C.G.A. Title 40, Chapter 2. You should request these records directly from the Georgia DOT, as this information will not be present in the Federal system.

---

[121] 49 C.F.R. § 387.33.
[122] 49 USC § 14504a(f).

4.6 What Are the Applicable Safety Standards?

All interstate carriers, except for those specifically exempted by statute, must comply with the minimum safety-fitness standards laid out in the FMCSR.[123]

> **Pro Note:** The Federal safety fitness standards closely track the Public Safety Transportation Rulebook put out by the Georgia Department of Transportation.[124]

The Federal repository for the safety review information and ratings are discussed below.

4.6.1 What Is a Safety Review?

Motor carriers are subject to compliance reviews to ensure compliance with safety standards. Pursuant to statute, the FMCSA conducts a safety review and issues a safety rating only after an in-person inspection.[125] The statute outlines many of the safety fitness standards used to determine the safety rating.[126]

The goal of the in-person evaluation for a safety rating is to determine if the motor carrier can demonstrate "it has adequate safety management controls in place, which function effectively to ensure acceptable compliance" with the regulations.[127] The FMCSA reviews the following issues to determine if the motor carrier meets the safety standards:

(a) Commercial driver's license standard violations (part 383),

---

[123] 49 C.F.R. § 385.1(d).
[124] Ga. Dep't Pub. Safety Website https://dps.georgia.gov/georgia-department-public-safety-transportation-rulebook (last accessed, Feb. 8, 2023).
[125] FMSCA Website https://csa.fmcsa.dot.gov/safetyplanner/MyFiles/Chapters.aspx?ch=20 (last accessed Feb. 8, 2023), (FMSCA website).
[126] 49 C.F.R. § 385.5.
[127] Id.

(b) Inadequate levels of financial responsibility (part 387),

(c) The use of unqualified drivers (part 391),

(d) Improper use and driving of motor vehicles (part 392),

(e) Unsafe vehicles operating on the highways (part 393),

(f) Failure to maintain accident registers and copies of accident reports (part 390),

(g) The use of fatigued drivers (part 395),

(h) Inadequate inspection, repair, and maintenance of vehicles (part 396),

(i) Transportation of hazardous materials, driving and parking rule violations (part 397),

(j) Violation of hazardous materials regulations (parts 170-177), and

(k) Motor vehicle accidents and hazardous materials incidents.[128]

The fewer violations of these factors, the more likely a positive safety rating.

When determining the safety fitness rating, the FMCSA may consider the following information: (i) safety reviews, (ii) compliance reviews, and (iii) "**any other data**."[129] This is a broad definition. The FMCSR list certain factors that can be considered, including the following:

- safety management controls,

- frequency and severity of regulatory violations,

---

[128] 49 C.F.R. § 385.5.
[129] 49 C.F.R. § 385.7.

- frequency and severity of driver or vehicle regulatory violations identified during roadside inspections,

- the number and frequency of out-of-service driver or vehicle violations of motor carrier operations in commerce,

- increases or decreases of similar types of regulatory violations discovered during safety or compliance reviews,

- frequency of accidents; hazardous materials incidents; accident rate per million miles; indicators of preventable accidents; and whether such accidents, hazardous materials incidents, and preventable accident indicators have increased or declined over time, and

- number and severity of violations of CMV and motor safety rules, regulations, standards, and orders that are both issued by a State, Canada, or Mexico and compatible with Federal rules, regulations, standards, and orders.[130]

4.6.2 What Is a Safety Rating?

The FMCSA conducts a compliance review for a motor carrier, which results in a safety rating.[131] There are three potential ratings, as follows:

- *"Satisfactory"* "mean[ing] that a motor carrier has in place and functioning adequate safety management controls to meet the safety fitness standard prescribed in § 385.5."[132] For safety management controls to be sufficient, they must be "appropriate for the size and type of operation of the particular motor carrier."[133]

---

[130] 49 C.F.R. § 385.7.
[131] FMSCA Website https://csa.fmcsa.dot.gov/safetyplanner/MyFiles/Chapters.aspx?ch=20 (last accessed Feb. 8, 2023).
[132] 49 C.F.R. § 385.3.
[133] Id.

- *"Conditional"* "mean[ing that] a motor carrier does not have adequate safety management controls in place to ensure compliance with the safety fitness standard...."[134] As a result, these failures "<u>could</u> result in compliance issues identified in § 385.5, as articulated above."[135]

- *"Unsatisfactory"* "means a motor carrier does not have adequate safety management controls in place to ensure compliance with the safety fitness standard."[136] As a result, these failures <u>have already</u> "resulted" in compliance issues identified in § 385.5, as articulated above.[137]

As you can see, the difference between a conditional and unsatisfactory rating is whether or not the articulated failures have already resulted in compliance issues.

A carrier's rating is available to the public upon request. However, "[a]ny person requesting the assigned rating of a motor carrier shall provide the FMCSA with the motor carrier's name, principal office address, and, if known, the USDOT number or the docket number, if any."[138]

In the event a carrier receives a conditional rating, the FMCSA requires that the points of failure be remedied within a specified period. An unsatisfactory rating means that the carrier is prohibited from operating.[139] In this case, the carrier may request another review from the FMCSA after addressing the issues.[140]

In our prior work as defense attorneys for trucking companies, we assisted in appealing and removing conditional or unsatisfactory ratings.

---

[134] Id.
[135] Id. (emphasis supplied).
[136] Id.
[137] Id. (emphasis supplied).
[138] 49 C.F.R. § 385.19(b).
[139] FMCSA Website, https://csa.fmcsa.dot.gov/safetyplanner/MyFiles/SubSections.aspx?ch=20& sec=58&sub=103 (last accessed Feb. 17, 2023).
[140] 49 C.F.R. § 385.15.

The process, from our experience, involves correspondence from the FMCSA concerning the specific deficiencies that must be remedied. Following this correspondence, the motor carrier is allowed a set period of time to demonstrate that the deficiencies have been appropriately cured.

> **Pro Note:** A wise attorney will request any documents related to deficiency notices, including any correspondences concerning the deficiencies or remedies.

4.6.3 Where Is All of this Information Stored?

When analyzing a trucking claim, an experienced truck accident lawyer will likely review at least three government sources of information concerning a motor carrier. Safety information is generally stored in any of the following:

- Motor Carrier Management Information System (MCMIS),

- Safety and Fitness Electronic Records (SAFER), or

- Safety Measurement System (SMS)

The following sections discuss these in detail.

4.6.3.A What Is the Motor Carrier Management Information System (MCMIS)?

The FMCSA maintains the Motor Carrier Management Information System (MCMIS) as a repository for the collection and maintenance of records on the safety fitness of commercial motor carriers.[141] The

---

[141] FMCSA Website, https://ask.fmcsa.dot.gov/app/mcmiscatalog/c_chap1 (last accessed Feb. 17, 2023).

repository contains numerous types of records and data concerning motor carriers. This includes, but is not limited to, information related to crashes, motor carriers, and vehicle or driver inspections.[142]

The information can be somewhat overwhelming. The crash material, for example, includes "commercial vehicle crashes reported to the FMCSA...from the years 1989 to present." The information can be filtered by carrier name, DOT number, location etc., to assist in providing a more useful data set.[143] This system can be accessed by Federal and state users as well as the motor carrier industry, law enforcement, and the general public. If you need further help on efficiently researching this system, we are here to help.

> **Pro Note:** The FMCSA maintains detailed crash information for commercial motor vehicles from 1989 to present. This catalog and information can be found on the FMCSA website.[144]

4.6.3.B What Is the Safety and Fitness Electronic Records (SAFER) System?

The FMCSA created The Safety and Fitness Electronic Records (SAFER) System as a repository of information about motor carriers.[145] When handling an accident involving a commercial motor vehicle, you should obtain a report of the safety review and rating. The SAFER system is available to the public.

The SAFER System provides public access to Carrier Snapshots, "a concise electronic record of a carrier's identification, size, commodity

---

[142] FMCSA Website, https://ask.fmcsa.dot.gov/app/mcmiscatalog/c_chap3 (last accessed Feb. 17, 2023).

[143] Id.

[144] FMCSA Website, https://ask.fmcsa.dot.gov/app/mcmiscatalog/mcmishome (last accessed Feb. 17, 2023).

[145] FMCSA Website, https://safer.fmcsa.dot.gov (last accessed Feb. 17, 2023).

information, and safety record, including safety rating (if any) and roadside out-of-service inspection information."[146] The SAFER website is easy to use and search. You can access the SAFER system online to review information on the motor carrier.[147]

4.6.3.C What Is the Safety Measurement System (SMS)?

The FMCSA also compiles data in the Safety Measurement System (SMS). The SMS includes information from the previous 24 months and is used by the FMCSA "to identify and intervene with motor carriers that pose the greatest risk to safety."[148] The information is compiled from roadside inspections, crash reports, and investigations.[149]

This information, in full, is available for enforcement purposes and for motor carriers. But, it is not open to the general public.[150] This distinguishes the SMS from SAFER and MCMIS systems. Certain information may be available to the public upon request.[151] You may access the SMS on the FMCSA's website.[152]

4.6.4 What Are the FMCSA Standards for Evaluating Safety (BASIC 7)?

The safety-related data collected by the FMCSA is segmented into seven categories, known as BASIC (Behavior Analysis and Safety Improvement Categories) categories. These categories are used to

---

[146] FMCSA Website, https://safer.fmcsa.dot.gov/about.aspx (last accessed Feb. 17, 2023).
[147] Id.
[148] FMCSA Website, https://csa.fmcsa.dot.gov/about/Measure (last accessed Feb. 17, 2023).
[149] Id.
[150] Id.
[151] Id.
[152] FMCSA Website, https://ai.fmcsa.dot.gov/sms/ (last accessed Feb. 17, 2023).

determine a motor carrier's performance as compared with other motor carriers.[153] The BASIC categories include:

- *Unsafe Driving* — This factor addresses unsafe driving behavior, such as texting, speeding, reckless driving, and more.

- *Crash Indicator* — This factor includes the "last two years" of state-reported crashes.

- *Hours of Service* — This factor primarily concerns fatigued and overworked drivers, where there are violations of the Hours-Of-Service (HOS) regulations.

- *Vehicle Maintenance* — This factor concerns the compliance of the motor carrier and drivers with necessary inspections and maintenance duties.

- *Controlled Substances/Alcohol* — This factor addresses the use of alcohol and drugs (illegal and legal) while operating a commercial motor vehicle.

- *Hazardous Materials* — This factor concerns the FMCSR for proper transportation of hazardous materials.

- *Driver Fitness* — This factor includes compliance with the driver qualification standards of the FMCSR.[154]

The BASICs are stored in the SMS system. As discussed above, not all of this information is publicly available. In particular, the crash indicator and hazardous material compliance are not available to the public.[155] Feel free to reach out to us with any questions about records requests and search processes.

---

[153] FMCSA Website, https://csa.fmcsa.dot.gov/Documents/CSA_GRS_Visor_S.pdf (last accessed Feb. 17, 2023).
[154] Id.
[155] Id.

4.7 What Is an Accident Register?

Motor carriers are legally required to maintain an accident register.[156] The register must include "3 years" of information.[157] The volume of information in the register may vary, but "[t]he register must contain, at minimum, the date of the crash, the city or town and state most near where the crash occurred, the driver's name, the number of injuries or fatalities, and whether hazardous materials, other than fuel spilled from the fuel tanks of motor vehicle involved in the crash, were released."[158]

While this and other government-collected material may seem invaluable to the investigation of a truck accident, it may not be discoverable. Federal law contains a privilege for certain information, stating "[n]o part of a report of an accident occurring in operations of a motor carrier, motor carrier of migrant workers, or motor private carrier and required by the Secretary, and no part of a report of an investigation of the accident made by the Secretary, may be admitted into evidence or used in a civil action for damages related to a matter mentioned in the report or investigation."[159] This is a broadly worded Federal privilege. At least one court has held that the Accident Register "is protected by statutory privilege" and not discoverable.[160]

> **Pro Note:** The objective of the Federal statutory privilege for many of the records used by the FMCSA is to permit open communication between the FMCSA and the motor carrier. It is important to understand this privilege and how it may impact discovery.

---

[156] 49 C.F.R. § 390.15.
[157] 49 C.F.R. § 390.15(b).
[158] FMCSA Website, https://csa.fmcsa.dot.gov/safetyplanner/MyFiles/SubSections.aspx?ch=21& sec=62&sub=127 (last accessed Feb. 17, 2023).
[159] 49 U.S.C.S. § 504(f).
[160] Sajda v. Brewton, 265 F.R.D. 334 (N.D. Ind. 2009).

4.8 What Are the Requirements for Hiring and Investigating Drivers?

A motor carrier regulated by the FMCSA is required to carry out a pre-employment screening of all of its drivers when hiring.[161] A number of these items must be complete prior to allowing them to drive.

4.8.1 What Type of Application Is Submitted by a Commercial Driver?

A truck driver is required to submit a written application for employment with the motor carrier.[162] The application records will show relevant information prior to employment with the motor carrier. The written application includes: (a) 3 years of prior addresses; (b) CDL license information; (c) experience with commercial motor vehicles; (d) list of all current and former CDLs; (e) 3 years of prior accidents; (f) any information regarding denial, suspension or revocation of their license; and (g) 3 years of prior employers, if not applying to drive a truck, and 10 years of prior employers if driving a truck.[163] Please note that different rules may be applicable for applications to transport hazardous materials, as defined in 49 C.F.R. § 383.

The application is certified as true and correct. As the regulations require the applicant to sign the following certification:

> *This certifies that this application was completed by me, and that all entries on it and information in it are true and complete to the best of my knowledge.*
>
> *(Date)*
>
> *(Applicant's signature)[164]*

---

[161] 49 C.F.R. § 391.

[162] 49 C.F.R. § 391.21(b).

[163] 49 C.F.R. § 391.21(b).

[164] 49 C.F.R. § 391.21(b)(12).

A truck accident attorney should review the driver's application and related records to make certain all of this information was collected, and any red flags are noted. If a motor carrier failed to collect relevant information or disregarded relevant red flags in these records, it may lead to direct liability on the part of the carrier. We discuss direct liability actions further in the Manual.

4.8.2 What Investigation Does the Motor Carrier Perform Upon Receipt of the Certified, Written Application from the Commercial Driver?

The trucking company is required to complete an investigation into the driver. The inquiry includes multiple parts. *One*, a motor carrier must obtain a moving violations report (also called a motor vehicle report or "MVR") from the state licensing authorities where the driver has held a license within the past 3 years.[165] *Two*, the motor carrier must verify prior employment with DOT-covered employers for the prior three years. This request may be written or oral (with documentation to support the request). The inquiry is focused on accidents and alcohol/drug tests.[166]

The responses to these inquiries "must be placed in the driver qualification file within 30 days of the date the driver's employment begins" and be maintained as required by Federal law.[167] Although the motor carrier has to inquire with prior DOT employers about the driver's history, there is not a reciprocal requirement that the former employer respond. Therefore, proof of the inquiry satisfies the rule. The driver qualification file is discussed, *supra*. It contains important information concerning the driver.

---

[165] 49 C.F.R. § 391.23.
[166] Id.
[167] Id.

4.8.3 What Is the FMCSA's Pre-Employment Screening Process?

In 2010, the FMCSA developed an electronic system to assist commercial drivers and motor carriers with monitoring the safety performance of a driver, which is called the Pre-Employment Screening Program or "PSP" for short.[168] This is a "voluntary program," and inquiry into a driver's PSP is <u>not</u> required when hiring. The PSP record "contains a driver's most recent 5 years of crash data and the most recent 3 years of roadside inspection data from the FMCSA MCMIS database."[169]

Title 49 of the U.S. Code, Section 31150, titled "Safety performance history screening," requires FMCSA to make certain crash and inspection data contained in the Motor Carrier Management Information System (MCMIS) electronically available for the purposes of conducting pre-employment screening.[170] While this information sounds helpful to a litigator, it is only accessible to authorized individuals, such as a motor carrier evaluating a driver for employment.[171] Therefore, any request for this information will need to be made to the motor carrier directly during the course of litigation.

> **Pro Note:** The report or older versions may be stored with the commercial motor carrier. Any such copy is likely not restricted and should be specifically requested.

4.8.4 Physical Examination of a Commercial Driver

The physical state of the driver is often a relevant factor in a CMV accident. The motor carrier must ensure that the driver has been certified as physically fit to operate a commercial motor vehicle by a medical examiner.[172] The medical examiner is required to be registered

---

[168] FMSCA Website, PSP, https://www.psp.fmcsa.dot.gov/psp/FAQ (last accessed Feb. 25, 2023).
[169] <u>Id.</u>
[170] 49 USC § 31150.
[171] <u>Id.</u>
[172] 49 C.F.R. § 391.23(m).

and approved to perform an examination of the driver.[173] The medical examiner must be "knowledgeable of the specific physical and mental demands associated with operating a commercial motor vehicle."[174]

In the application process, the commercial driver submits the medical examination certificate to the motor carrier. The motor carrier, in turn, verifies the examiner is properly registered to conduct the exam.[175]

The medical examiner's certificate appears like this:

| Form MCSA-5875 | | | OMB No.: 2126-0006 |

Last Name: _____ First Name: _____ DOB: _____ Exam Date: _____

Please complete only one of the following (Federal or State) Medical Examiner Determination sections:

MEDICAL EXAMINER DETERMINATION (Federal)

Use this section for examinations performed in accordance with the Federal Motor Carrier Safety Regulations (49 CFR 391.41-391.49):

○ Does not meet standards *(specify reason)*: _____
○ Meets standards in 49 CFR 391.41; qualifies for 2-year certificate
○ Meets standards, but periodic monitoring required *(specify reason)*: _____
   Driver qualified for: ○ 3 months ○ 6 months ○ 1 year ○ other *(specify)*: _____
   ☐ Wearing corrective lenses   ☐ Wearing hearing aid   ☐ Accompanied by a waiver/exemption *(specify type)*: _____
   ☐ Accompanied by a Skill Performance Evaluation (SPE) Certificate   ☐ Qualified by operation of 49 CFR 391.64 *(Federal)*
   ☐ Driving within an exempt intracity zone *(see 49 CFR 391.62) (Federal)*
○ Determination pending *(specify reason)*: _____
   ☐ Return to medical exam office for follow-up on *(must be 45 days or less)*: _____
   ☐ Medical Examination Report amended *(specify reason)*: _____
      (if amended) Medical Examiner's Signature: _____ Date: _____
○ Incomplete examination *(specify reason)*: _____

If the driver meets the standards outlined in 49 CFR 391.41, then complete a Medical Examiner's Certificate as stated in 49 CFR 391.43(h), as appropriate.

I have performed this evaluation for certification. I have personally reviewed all available records and recorded information pertaining to this evaluation, and attest that, to the best of my knowledge, I believe it to be true and correct.

Medical Examiner's Signature: _____
Medical Examiner's Name *(please print or type)*: _____
Medical Examiner's Address: _____ City: _____ State: _____ Zip Code: _____
Medical Examiner's Telephone Number: _____ Date Certificate Signed: _____
Medical Examiner's State License, Certificate, or Registration Number: _____ Issuing State: _____
☐ MD ☐ DO ☐ Physician Assistant ☐ Chiropractor ☐ Advanced Practice Nurse
☐ Other Practitioner *(specify)*: _____
National Registry Number: _____ | Medical Examiner's Certificate Expiration Date: [_____]

176

In litigation, when the driver's health is at issue, the full medical examination report can be important in determining if the driver was fit for duty. Discovering that a driver misrepresented his/her health condition in order to become certified may be a valuable piece of evidence in such

---

[173] 49 C.F.R. § 391.43.
[174] Id.
[175] 49 C.F.R. § 391.23(m).
[176] 49 C.F.R. § 391.43.

a case. The full inquiry will include a certification by the driver as to everything from anxiety and alcohol abuse to neck and back problems. We have seen a number of cases where the driver failed to properly list a medical condition that arguably contributed to the incident, such as a sleep disorder leading to drowsiness.

A picture of a portion of the inquiry is as follows:

Form MCSA-5875				OMB No.: 2126-0006			

Last Name:	First Name:	DOB:	Exam Date:

DRIVER HEALTH HISTORY *(continued)*

Do you have or have you ever had:	Yes	No	Not Sure		Yes	No	Not Sure
1. Head/brain injuries or illnesses *(e.g., concussion)*	○	○	○	16. Dizziness, headaches, numbness, tingling, or memory loss	○	○	○
2. Seizures/epilepsy	○	○	○	17. Unexplained weight loss	○	○	○
3. Eye problems *(except glasses or contacts)*	○	○	○	18. Stroke, mini-stroke (TIA), paralysis, or weakness	○	○	○
4. Ear and/or hearing problems	○	○	○	19. Missing or limited use of arm, hand, finger, leg, foot, toe	○	○	○
5. Heart disease, heart attack, bypass, or other heart problems	○	○	○	20. Neck or back problems	○	○	○
6. Pacemaker, stents, implantable devices, or other heart procedures	○	○	○	21. Bone, muscle, joint, or nerve problems	○	○	○
7. High blood pressure	○	○	○	22. Blood clots or bleeding problems	○	○	○
8. High cholesterol	○	○	○	23. Cancer	○	○	○
9. Chronic (long-term) cough, shortness of breath, or other breathing problems	○	○	○	24. Chronic (long-term) infection or other chronic diseases	○	○	○
10. Lung disease *(e.g., asthma)*	○	○	○	25. Sleep disorders, pauses in breathing while asleep, daytime sleepiness, loud snoring	○	○	○
11. Kidney problems, kidney stones, or pain/problems with urination	○	○	○	26. Have you ever had a sleep test *(e.g., sleep apnea)*?	○	○	○
12. Stomach, liver, or digestive problems	○	○	○	27. Have you ever spent a night in the hospital?	○	○	○
13. Diabetes or blood sugar problems	○	○	○	28. Have you ever had a broken bone?	○	○	○
Insulin used	○	○	○	29. Have you ever used or do you now use tobacco?	○	○	○
				30. Do you currently drink alcohol?	○	○	○
14. Anxiety, depression, nervousness, other mental health problems	○	○	○	31. Have you used an illegal substance within the past two years?	○	○	○
15. Fainting or passing out	○	○	○	32. Have you ever failed a drug test or been dependent on an illegal substance?	○	○	○

Other health condition(s) not described above: ○ Yes ○ No ○ Not Sure

Did you answer "yes" to any of questions 1-32? If so, please comment further on those health conditions below: ○ Yes ○ No ○ Not Sure

(Attach additional sheets if necessary)

CMV DRIVER'S SIGNATURE

I certify that the above information is accurate and complete. I understand that inaccurate, false or missing information may invalidate the examination and my Medical Examiner's Certificate, that submission of fraudulent or intentionally false information is a violation of 49 CFR 390.35, and that submission of fraudulent or intentionally false information may subject me to civil or criminal penalties under 49 CFR 390.37 and 49 CFR 386 Appendices A and B.

Driver's Signature: Date:

SECTION 2. Examination Report *(to be filled out by the medical examiner)*

DRIVER HEALTH HISTORY REVIEW

Review and discuss pertinent driver answers and any available medical records. Comment on the driver's responses to the "health history" questions that may affect the driver's safe operation of a commercial motor vehicle (CMV).

(Attach additional sheets if necessary)

Page 2

177

---

[177] Id.

> **Pro Note:** The medical exam includes a detailed health history of the driver that the driver certifies as accurate. Make certain you have a medical expert review any reported health issues for potential connections with drowsiness or other symptoms potentially giving rise to an accident.

The goal of the medical exam is to ensure that the driver meets the FMCSR as it relates to physical fitness. This includes that the driver is physically fit enough to safely perform functions as a driver.[178] The driver is also examined for mental fitness.[179] This information can be crucial to developing your case.

4.8.5 Is There a Requirement that the Motor Carrier Examines the Driver's Skills Over the Road?

To operate a tractor-trailer, a driver must obtain a Commercial Driver's License (CDL).[180] Each state's rules for licensure vary slightly. As our practice is based in Georgia, we will focus on the Georgia rules.

In Georgia, as in many states, a CDL driver must demonstrate competency in operating a commercial vehicle by passing a skills test. The skills test includes parallel parking, backing, using the clutch, turning, and other road skills—all while operating a tractor-trailer.[181]

If the driver has passed a road test by a state licensing authority, then there is no requirement that the motor carrier perform further road testing. "In place of, and as equivalent to, the road test required by §391.31, a person who seeks to drive a commercial motor vehicle may present, and a motor carrier may accept...[a] valid Commercial Driver's License as

---

[178] 49 C.F.R. § 391.43(g)(2).
[179] 49 C.F.R. § 391.45(g).
[180] FMCSA Website, CDL License, https://www.fmcsa.dot.gov/registration/commercial-drivers-license (last accessed Feb. 25, 2023).
[181] Georgia Dep't of Driver's Services Website, CDL Road Test, https://dds.georgia.gov/testing-and-training/test-and-exams-information#road.

defined in §383.5 of this subchapter." (Note: A basic CDL license does not include double/triple trailer or tank vehicle endorsements.)[182]

While a road test is not required, some commercial motor carriers still perform a road test of their drivers at the time of hiring or pursuant to annual inspection. This inquiry may reveal issues giving rise to an accident. In one prior case, we discovered a prior road test in which the commercial driver failed the backing portion of the exam. The cause, in our case, also concerned backing. This was helpful evidence in pushing the case to resolution.

> **Pro Note:** A road test is generally not required by the FMCSR. However, some motor carriers still perform them. These tests can contain important information about the driver's abilities, as examined by the carrier.

4.9 Obtaining a CDL

Per the FMCSA, in order to operate certain types of commercial vehicles, a commercial driver must have a valid commercial driver's license ("CDL"). Ironically, some vehicles that are classified as commercial vehicles (i.e., GVWR in excess of 10,000lbs) may not actually require a CDL.[183] However, for purposes of this section, we will assume the GVWR of the vehicle is such that it requires a CDL.

Generally, CDLs authorize the driver to drive under specific weight and vehicle combinations. The basic classes of CDL are divided into the following groupings:

---

[182] 49 C.F.R. 391.33.
[183] FMCSA, Exemptions to the Federal Motor Carrier Safety Regulations https://www.fmcsa.dot.gov/registration/commercial-drivers-license/driver-combination-vehicle-gcwr-less-26001-pounds-required (last accessed Mar. 1, 2023).

- *Group A* - Any combination of vehicles with a GVWR in excess of 26,000 lbs., provided the GVWR of the vehicle(s) being towed is in excess of 10,000 lbs.

- *Group B* - Any single vehicle with a GVWR in excess of 26,000 lbs., or any vehicle towing a vehicle not in excess of 10,000 lbs.

- *Group C* - Any vehicles not covered in Group A or B which is designed to transport 16 or more passengers or is used in transporting hazardous materials.[184]

4.9.1 A Commercial Learner's Permit (CLP)

Similar to the process for obtaining a civilian license, a commercial driver may obtain a commercial learner's permit (CLP) prior to obtaining a CDL.[185] The CLP can be issued after the driver successfully completes the written examination and passes a DOT medical examination.[186] A CLP does not require a road test.[187]

The written examination is based on the FMCSR and, in particular, the Commercial Driver's Manual of the state in question.[188] The State of Georgia's manual is available on its website. The CDL manual contains information that the driver needs to know to pass their licensing examination. For truck crash attorneys, this manual is a source of information used in establishing the standard of care to which a professional driver should be held in operating the commercial vehicle.[189]

---

[184] FMCSA Website, CDL, https://www.fmcsa.dot.gov/registration/commercial-drivers-license/drivers (last accessed Mar. 1, 2023) Georgia Dep't of Driver Services, License Classes, https://dds.georgia.gov/license-classes (last accessed Mar. 1, 2023).
[185] FMCSA Website, How to Obtain a CDL, https://www.fmcsa.dot.gov/registration/commercial-drivers-license/how-do-i-get-commercial-drivers-license (last accessed Mar. 1, 2023).
[186] Id.
[187] Id.
[188] Id.
[189] The Georgia manual is available at: https://dds.georgia.gov/dds-forms-and-manuals/manuals (last accessed Aug. 4, 2023).

Unlike a traditional learner's permit, which may be held for months, a CLP is only required to be held for 14 days. During this 14-day period, the driver is permitted "to practice on public roads with a qualified CDL holder sitting next to" them.[190] Following this 14-day period, the driver may apply for their CDL. Before the CDL can be issued, the driver must pass a skills test, which includes a test of over-the-road driving skills.[191]

4.9.2 Entry-Level Drivers

There are special requirements in place for new (inexperienced) drivers. These drivers must complete entry-level driver training (often referred to as ELDT). Entry-level driver training includes training on (a) "driver qualification materials," (b) "hours of service of drivers," (c) "driver wellness," and (d) "whistleblower protection."[192]

The training must come from an entity listed on FMCSA's Training Provider Registry.[193] Upon completion of the training, the driver receives a "training certificate" as proof of completion of the required training.[194] In the event a motor carrier utilizes an entry-level driver, then the motor carrier "must ensure the driver has received a training certificate containing all the information contained in § 380.513 from the training provider."[195]

Remember, while the FMCSR expressly include a training requirement for entry-level drivers, there is no such express requirement for fully licensed drivers.[196]

---

[190] Id.
[191] Id.
[192] 49 C.F.R. § 380.503.
[193] 49 C.F.R. 380.609(a) ; 49 C.F.R. § 380.700 *et seq.*
[194] 49 C.F.R. § 380.717.
[195] 49 C.F.R. § 380.505.
[196] Ortiz v. Wiwi, 2012 U.S. Dist. LEXIS 137881 at *12 (M.D. Ga. 2012).

4.9.3 Additional Endorsements to CDL

A CDL may have special rights or privileges based upon the endorsements present.[197] This is true for multi-trailer setups, passenger vehicles, tankers, school buses, and vehicles hauling hazardous materials.[198]

Each endorsement will, of course, contain rules and regulations applicable to it. For example, the regulations place additional training requirements on "longer combination vehicles (LCV)" which include "any combination of a truck-tractor and two or more trailers or semi-trailers, which operate on the National System of Interstate and Defense Highways with a gross vehicle weight (GVW) greater than 36,288 kilograms (80,000 pounds)."[199]

To receive an endorsement, the driver must generally demonstrate specific skills as part of a written test, road test, or a combination thereof. The following chart can assist in determining if a potential endorsement is applicable to your case:

---

[197] FMCSA, Website, CDL Endorsements, https://www.fmcsa.dot.gov/registration/commercial-drivers-license/drivers (last accessed Mar. 1, 2023).
[198] Id.
[199] 49 C.F.R. § 380.105(b).

Endorsement code	Description
T	Double/Triple Trailers (Knowledge test only)
P*	Passenger (Knowledge and Skills Tests)
N	Tank vehicle (Knowledge test only)
H*	Hazardous materials (Knowledge test only)
X	Combination of tank vehicle and hazardous materials endorsements (Knowledge test only)
S*	School Bus (Knowledge and Skills Tests)
CLP Endorsements - Only 3 endorsements are allowed on the CLP	
P	Passenger, A CLP holder with a "P" endorsement is prohibited from operating a CMV carrying passengers, other than Federal/state auditors and inspectors, test examiners, other trainees, and the CDL holder accompanying the CLP holder as prescribed by 49CFR383.25(a)(1).
S	School Bus, A CLP holder with an "S" endorsement is prohibited from operating a school with passengers, other than Federal/state auditors and inspectors, test examiners, other trainees, and the CDL holder accompanying the CLP holder as prescribed by 49CFR383.25(a)(1).
N	Tank Endorsement, A CLP holder with an "N" endorsement may only operate an empty tank vehicle, and is prohibited from operating any tank vehicle that previously contained hazardous materials that have not been purged of any residue.

200

4.10 Transporting Hazardous Materials

The FMCSR place special requirements (above and beyond the other generally-applicable FMCSR provisions) on carriers and drivers who transport hazardous materials. A driver must obtain a special endorsement to transport such materials.[201] The FMCSR dedicate 49 C.F.R. § 397 *et seq.* to the transportation of hazardous materials.[202] These provisions will

---

[200] FMCSA, Website, CDL Endorsements, https://www.fmcsa.dot.gov/registration/commercial-drivers-license/drivers (last accessed Mar. 1, 2023).
[201] Id.
[202] 49 C.F.R. § 397.

likely be relevant provisions to any accident involving transportation of hazardous materials.

The rules define "hazardous materials" to include radioactive, explosive, poisonous, and flammable materials.[203] The motor carrier is required to obtain an appropriate safety permit to transport these materials.[204] The motor carrier must also have a "satisfactory" rating and <u>not</u> be in the top 30% of motor carriers for crash rate to obtain such a permit.[205]

Once the permit is secured, the transportation of hazardous materials subjects the driver and motor carrier to numerous other regulations, both general and specific to certain chemicals.[206]

In cases involving the transportation of hazardous materials, it is advisable to consult with an expert in the particular hazardous waste at issue to determine if the motor carrier transported the hazardous material properly. We have experience with motor carriers that transport hazardous waste and connections with experts in that field. Don't hesitate to reach out to us if you need assistance.

4.11 Federal Minimum Standards for Driver Qualifications

Under the FMCSA, a driver must meet numerous qualifications to operate a commercial vehicle in interstate commerce. Georgia has adopted this same standard.

The following are the minimum requirements:

- Be at least 21 years of age.[207]

---

[203] 49 C.F.R. § 385.403.
[204] Id.
[205] 49 C.F.R. § 385.407.
[206] See 49 C.F.R. § 397 et seq.
[207] 49 C.F.R. § 391.11.

> **Pro Note:** If the truck is not transporting hazardous materials, a truck driver engaged in <u>intrastate</u> commerce may be 18 years of age.[208]

- Speak and read English satisfactorily to:

  o Converse with the general public;

  o Understand traffic signs and signals;

  o Respond to official questions; and

  o Make legible entries on reports and records.[209]

- Drive the vehicle safely.

- Be physically qualified to perform all duties of a driver.

- Have only one valid commercial motor vehicle operator's license issued by one State or jurisdiction.

- Pass a driver's road test or equivalent.[210]

Motor carriers must ensure and verify that their CMV drivers meet the minimum requirements specified in 49 C.F.R. § 391 before operating a vehicle.[211] There is an exception to certain investigation requirements if a driver is employed by multiple motor carriers and the driver has been actively employed by another motor carrier within the prior 7-day period.[212]

---

[208] 49 C.F.R. 383.71.
[209] 49 C.F.R. § 391.11.
[210] Id.
[211] 49 C.F.R. § 391.11.
[212] 49 C.F.R. § 391.63.

> **Pro Note:** CMV owner–operators must comply with the rules that apply to motor carriers <u>and</u> the rules that apply to drivers. An owner–operator is a person who operates a CMV under his or her own authority (U.S. DOT Number) as both a motor carrier and self-employed driver.[213]

4.12 Disqualification of a Driver

"Disqualified" means a driver cannot legally operate a commercial motor vehicle. In particular, 49 C.F.R. § 391.15 enumerates certain acts that "disqualify" a driver. These include: (a) a suspended, revoked, or withdrawn license; (b) operating a commercial motor vehicle while under the influence of alcohol (defined as .04 or more); (c) operating a commercial motor vehicle while under the influence of any Schedule 1 controlled substance; (d) transporting any Schedule 1 controlled substance; (e) performing a hit and run; or (f) committing a felony using a motor vehicle.[214]

The disqualification is generally temporary. For a driver with a suspended/revoked/withdrawn license, the driver is disqualified for the duration of the suspension. For a driver convicted of certain criminal offenses like drunk driving, the driver is generally disqualified for 1 year for a first offense. A driver who is convicted of <u>two</u> or more "texting while driving" offenses is disqualified for 60 days or more. These examples show that the period of disqualification varies significantly. 49 C.F.R. § 391.15 contains all of the dates of disqualification for various offenses.[215]

In addition, a driver may also be disqualified for violating an out-of-service order. The time period for the disqualification increases based on the number of violations within a specified time period.[216]

---

[213] FMCSA Website, Motor Carrier Safety Planner, https://csa.fmcsa.dot.gov/safetyplanner/MyFiles/Sections.aspx?ch=23&sec=66 (last accessed Mar. 3, 2023).
[214] 49 C.F.R. § 391.15.
[215] Id.
[216] Id.

The FMCSR contain helpful tables for determining the length of time of disqualification. These tables are divided into the following:

* Table 1: Disqualification for major offenses

* Table 2: Disqualification for serious traffic violations

* Table 3: Disqualification for railroad-highway grade crossing offenses.

* Table 4: Disqualification for violating out-of-service orders.[217]

We recommend reviewing these tables thoroughly.

One interesting aspect of these disqualifying provisions is that a driver is required to self-report in many instances. 49 C.F.R. § 333.33 provides that:

> *Each employee who has a driver's license suspended, revoked, or canceled by a State or jurisdiction, who loses the right to operate a commercial motor vehicle in a State or jurisdiction for any period, or who is disqualified from operating a commercial motor vehicle for any period, shall notify his/her current employer of such suspension, revocation, cancellation, lost privilege, or disqualification. The notification must be made before the end of the business day following the day the employee received notice of the suspension, revocation, cancellation, lost privilege, or disqualification.[218]*

If a driver fails to provide disqualifying information, this may be grounds for liability.

4.13 What Are the Requirements for Securing Cargo?

Different configurations of truck and trailer require varying levels of knowledge and skill concerning the loading and securing of cargo.

---

[217] 49 C.F.R. § 383.51.
[218] 49 C.F.R. § 333.33.

The FMCSR have specific requirements to "prevent cargo from leaking, spilling, blowing, or falling from a commercial vehicle."[219] The regulations also work to prevent cargo from moving or shifting in transport, which can lead to tipping.[220] There are regulations specific to general types of cargo as well.

The cargo securement regulations are found in 49 C.F.R. § 393.100 *et seq.* The general rule is that "[c]argo must be firmly immobilized or secured on or within a vehicle by structures of adequate strength, dunnage or dunnage bags, shoring bars, tiedowns or a combination of these."[221] If the cargo has a tendency to roll, it should be restrained by "chocks, wedges, a cradle, or other equivalent means to prevent rolling."[222] The restraints should be sufficiently placed to inhibit loosening during operation.

A tiedown must be fastened in a manner that secures the cargo. This means that adequately sized tiedowns must be used, as defined by their "working load limit."[223] The manufacturer generally assigns the working load limit for a tiedown.[224] The tiedowns must be secured to an "anchor point," a specific part of the structure intended to anchor a tiedown.[225] The number of tiedowns must also be proper. In general, the FMCSR require "one tiedown for articles 5 feet or less in length, and 1,100 pounds or less in weight."[226] For an object greater than 5 feet but less than 10 feet, two tiedowns must be used. An additional tiedown is required for every 10 feet of additional length beyond the first 10 feet, including any fraction over.[227]

---

[219] FMCA, Motor Carrier Safety Planner, https://csa.fmcsa.dot.gov/safetyplanner/MyFiles/SubSections.aspx?ch=22&sec=64&sub=132 (last accessed Mar. 3, 2023).
[220] Id.
[221] 49 C.F.R. § 393.106.
[222] Id. at (c)(1).
[223] Id.
[224] 49 C.F.R. § 393.5.
[225] Id.
[226] 49 C.F.R. § 393.110.
[227] Id.

These rules do not account for specific cargo, such as steel, which has specific regulations associated with it.[228] In a case we handled involving a steel hauling tractor-trailer, the weight of the steel was so great that it inhibited the truck's ability to properly stop, causing a massive collision. Cargo of this magnitude must be stored appropriately.

The following is a list of cargo that has specific regulations: (a) logs, (b) dressed lumber or similar building products, (c) metal coils, (d) paper rolls, (e) concrete pipes, (f) intermodal containers, (g) automobiles, light trucks, and vans, (h) heavy vehicles, equipment and machinery, (i) flattened or crushed vehicles, (j) roll-on/roll-off or hook lift containers, (k) and large boulders.[229] These regulations are too voluminous to discuss here. However, in any shifting cargo case, it is important to review the regulations to determine if any specific regulations apply.

In addition, there are specific regulations governing the loading and unloading of hazardous material, which are detailed and voluminous.[230] The basic rule is stated as follows — The FMCSR require any package containing hazardous materials, which is not permanently attached to a motor vehicle, to be adequately secured against shifting or moving within the transport vehicle under usual transportation conditions.[231] It is important to note that packages equipped with valves or fittings must be loaded in a manner that reduces the risk of damage during transportation.[232]

Compliance with these regulations is critical to ensure the safety of individuals and property, as well as to mitigate the risk of truck accidents caused by unsecured hazardous materials. Therefore, it is imperative for all trucking companies and drivers to adhere to these regulations to minimize the risk of accidents.

---

[228] Id.
[229] 49 C.F.R. § 393.116 to 136.
[230] 49 C.F.R. Part 177.
[231] 49 C.F.R. § 177.834(a).
[232] Id.

4.14 Investigation of Annual Driving Record

The rules contain requirements for both the motor carrier and the driver to audit the driver's record yearly.

4.14.1 Motor Carrier's Duty to Conduct Annual Review of Driving Record

A commercial motor carrier must complete an annual inspection or review (every 12 months) of a driver's driving record to determine whether the driver remains qualified.[233] These inquiries are made to the jurisdiction governing the driver's commercial motor vehicle license. Here is an example motor vehicle record ("MVR") report.

```
MOTOR VEHICLE RECORD
State: GA       License #: XXXXXXXX

**** END OF HISTORY       *****
------------------------- DRIVER INFORMATION ---------------------------------
Doe,John
123 ABC Street
XYZ City, Georgia

LICENSE : XXXXXXXX --------------------------------------------------------
TYPE: COMMERCIAL                                    ISSUED: 11/11/2111

  CLASS : A - COMBINE VEH > 26K W/TRAILER > 10K      EXPIRE: 11/11/2211
  STATUS: VALID
  ENDORSEMENTS: NONE
  NOTES : ORIGINAL ISSUE - 11/11/1111

NOTES:
ORIGINAL CDL ISSUE DATE: 11/11/1111
TOTAL STATE POINTS : 3


  TYPE        NON EXCEPTED INTERSTATE
  EFFECTIVE:

  --------------------------------------------------------------------------
  ITM TYPE       OCCURED CONV/REIN ST DESCRIPTION                      PTS
  --------- -------- --------    -------------------------------
    1 VIOLATION  11/11/11 11/11/11  GA A) Failure to Yield               3

    2 VIOLATION  11/11/11 11/11/11  GA A) FAILURE TO APPEAR              0

    3 VIOLATION  11/11/11 11/11/11  GA A) SPEEDING 20+ OVER THE LIMIT    3

                       *** END OF REPORT ***
```

---

[233] 49 C.F.R. § 391.25.

The MVR report is kept in the driver qualification file. "A copy of the motor vehicle record required by paragraph (a) of this section shall be maintained in the driver's qualification file."[234] The motor carrier must also review the MVR to determine if the driver meets the minimum requirements for driving.[235] The regulations are not entirely clear; but, they appear to give the motor carrier some discretion "to determine whether the driver meets minimum requirements for safe driving...."[236] The regulations advise the motor carrier to consider the driver's "accident record" and moving violations.[237]

4.14.2 Driver's Duty to Notify His Employer of Violations

Before a 2022 rule change, a driver had a duty to make an annual report of driving violations to his employer. This former rule was housed in 49 C.F.R. § 391.27. However, effective May 9, 2022, the FMCSA eliminated this requirement as duplicative of the motor carrier's annual inquiry into the commercial driver's MVR with the state's licensing authority.[238]

The newly implemented regulations, then, rely upon the motor carrier's annual inquiry *and* the commercial driver's obligation to inform the state authority and their employer about traffic convictions. 49 C.F.R. § 383.31 requires 30-days' notice of any convictions for violations of the rules of the road to the state agency governing a driver's licensure.[239] If the conviction occurs in a state that automatically reports citations to the licensing board, then the driver is in compliance with his or her reporting obligations.[240]

---

[234] 49 C.F.R. § 391.25(c)(1).
[235] 49 C.F.R. § 391.25(b).
[236] Id.
[237] Id.
[238] 87 F.R. 13192.
[239] 49 C.F.R. § 383.31(a).
[240] Id. at (d).

In addition to the above requirements, a commercial driver must also notify their employer of any convictions within 30 days.

> *Each person who operates a commercial motor vehicle, who has a commercial driver's license issued by a State or jurisdiction, and who is convicted of violating, in any type of motor vehicle, a State or local law relating to motor vehicle traffic control (other than a parking violation), shall notify his/her current employer of such conviction. The notification must be made within 30 days after the date that the person has been convicted.[241]*

4.15 The Driver Qualification File

One of the most important pieces of evidence in many truck accident cases is the driver qualification file. The regulations require a motor carrier to maintain a "Driver Qualification File" or "DQF."[242] The driver qualification file contains key information for the driver, demonstrating whether or not the motor carrier complied with the hiring and investigation requirements from the Federal Rules when employing a driver.

The DQF must contain the following records:

- Driver application,[243]

- Motor vehicle record(s) from the 3-year period prior to hiring date,[244]

- Certificate of road test (or equivalent),[245]

- Safety inquiry with prior employer(s),[246]

- (If applicable) Certificate of training for entry-level drivers,[247]

- Motor vehicle record from the prior 12 months,[248]

---

[241] Id. at (b).
[242] 49 C.F.R. § 391.51(a).
[243] 49 C.F.R. § 391.21.
[244] 49 C.F.R. § 391.23.
[245] 49 C.F.R. § 391.33.
[246] 49 C.F.R. § 391.23.
[247] 49 C.F.R. § 380.509.
[248] 49 C.F.R. § 391.25.

- Annual review by the motor carrier, and[249]

- Medical examiner's certificate for the driver.[250]

The driver's qualification file must be retained "for as long as a driver is employed by that motor carrier and for three years thereafter."[251] Certain records may be removed from a driver's qualification file after three years.[252]

There is an exception to the requirement to maintain a driver qualification file, when the carrier only employs the driver intermittently and the driver is employed by another carrier during the period in question. In such a case, the carrier can get a certification of compliance from the driver's other employer rather than maintain its own file on the driver.[253]

> **Pro Note:** The driver qualification file should be requested in discovery. The motor carrier ordinarily must maintain this file, and it may well contain relevant information.

This information can be helpful when asserting direct liability against a carrier for negligent hiring or entrustment. It is also helpful to determine the driver's fitness to serve. Also, this file is essential in the process of assessing a driver's qualifications.

4.16 Commercial Vehicle Insurance Requirements

The minimum liability coverage requirements for a commercial driver and motor carrier are unique to each state. In Georgia, for example, a motor vehicle must maintain automobile insurance with no less than $25,000 in bodily injury liability coverage per person and no less than $50,000 per accident.[254] There is no Federal law establishing the insurance requirements for non-commercial vehicles.

---

[249] 49 C.F.R. § 391.25.
[250] 49 C.F.R. § 391.43.
[251] 49 C.F.R. § 391.51(c).
[252] 49 C.F.R. § 391.51(d).
[253] 49 C.F.R. § 391.65.
[254] O.C.G.A. § 33-77-11(a).

However, Federal law does require commercial motor carriers to have insurance. The Federal rules for insurance requirements supersede the state regulations for insurance requirements for commercial motor vehicles.

> **Pro Note:** The requirement for insurance applies to the motor carrier and/or driver of the truck. This applies for leased or rented trucks as well. Often, the lessor will have a policy on the truck that names the lessee/driver as a permissive user.

As detailed in the registration section above, the FMCSR require that any motor carrier must file proof of liability insurance prior to operating.[255] The requirement for insurance is often called the motor carrier's proof of "financial responsibility." The minimum limits of "financial responsibility" depend on the type of activity performed. "The purpose of the Federal statute and regulations is to ensure that a [motor] carrier has independent financial responsibility to pay for losses sustained by the general public arising out of its trucking operations."[256]

The FMCSR have charts which are helpful in determining the minimum amount of coverage required for each activity. These charts are set forth below:

Type of carriage	Commodity transported	Minimum Limits
(1) For-hire (In interstate or foreign commerce, with a gross vehicle weight rating of 10,001 or more pounds)	Property (nonhazardous)	$750,000

---

[255] 49 C.F.R. § 387.31; 49 C.F.R. § 390.205.
[256] Travelers Ins. Co. V. Transport Ins. Co., 787 F.2d 1133, 1140 (7th Cir. 1986).

Type of carriage	Commodity transported	Minimum Limits
(2) For-hire and Private (In interstate, foreign, or intrastate commerce, with a gross vehicle weight rating of 10,001 or more pounds)	Hazardous substances, as defined in 49 C.F.R. 171.8, transported in bulk in cargo tanks, portable tanks, or hopper-type vehicles with capacities in bulk; in bulk Division 1.1, 1.2 or 1.3 materials; Division 2.3, Hazard Zone A material; in bulk Division 6.1, Packing Group I, Hazard Zone A material; in bulk Division 2.1 or 2.2 material; or highway route controlled quantities of a Class 7 material, as defined in 49 C.F.R. 173.403	5,000,000
(3) For-hire and Private (In interstate or foreign commerce, in any quantity; or in intrastate commerce, in bulk only; with a gross vehicle weight rating of 10,001 or more pounds)	Oil listed in 49 C.F.R. 172.101; hazardous waste, hazardous materials, or hazardous substances defined in 49 C.F.R. 171.8 and listed in 49 C.F.R. 172.101, but not mentioned in entry (2) or (4) of this table	1,000,000
(4) For-hire and Private (In interstate or foreign commerce, with a gross vehicle weight rating of less than 10,001 pounds)	In bulk Division 1.1, 1.2, or 1.3 material; in bulk Division 2.3, Hazard Zone A material; in bulk Division 6.1, Packing Group I, Hazard Zone A material; or highway route-controlled quantities of a Class 7 material as defined in 49 C.F.R. 173.403	5,000,000

257

The amounts differ for *passenger* carrying vehicles.

257 49 C.F.R. § 387.9.

Vehicle seating capacity	Minimum limits
(a) Any vehicle with a seating capacity of 16 passengers or more, including the driver	$5,000,000
(b) Any vehicle with a seating capacity of 15 passengers or less, including the driver	1,500,000

258

Motor carriers are not the only entities within the trucking industry required to carry substantial insurance. Brokers and freight forwarders must also carry minimum limits, prescribed by Federal law.[259] The regulations have helpful charts for these insurance requirements. Because these persons are not typically the main targets of a truck case, we are not repeating them here.

It is common for a motor carrier to have more than one insurance provider. Obtaining insurance records from the FMCSA may provide valuable early information in the settlement and negotiation process. It is important to note that trailer owners (if separate from the owner of the tractor) may also have a liability policy on the trailer. In some instances, this policy may be as large as the policy on commercial vehicles. The policy (or the MCS-90 endorsement) may treat the truck driver as a permissive user, have separate limits of coverage, and thus offer a second layer of insurance coverage in the event of an accident.

4.16.1 Financial Responsibility and Form MCS-90

The motor carrier maintains proof of "financial responsibility" through an insurer by maintaining a "Form MCS-90" issued by the insurer. The MCS-90 endorsement essentially requires that the insurer guarantee or stand as a surety for injuries to third parties, up to the amount of coverage provided, if the injury is not otherwise covered by the policy. The Form is executed by the insurer and provides (a) the amount of insurance, (b) if it is primary or excess coverage, and (c) the identifying information of the

---

[258] 49 C.F.R. § 387.33T.
[259] 49 C.F.R. § 387.303 & 387.303T (for brokers); 49 C.F.R. § 384.405 (freight forwarders).

insurer. The majority view of courts is that the MCS-90 creates a "surety" bond with the injured public, as opposed to mere insurance.[260] It serves as "a safety net in the event other insurance is lacking."[261] In other words, if there is no underlying insurance, the MCS-90 kicks in and provides coverage up to its stated amount.[262]

The underlying policy reason behind this requirement is to ensure there is compensation for an injured third party, when they are in a collision with a commercial motor vehicle. While the MCS-90 is not insurance coverage *per se*, it operates as a suretyship for the benefit of the public.[263] Therefore, the MCS-90 provides coverage when there is a policy exclusion that otherwise thwarts coverage, such as non-cooperation of the insured.[264] However, this does not mean that there is <u>more</u> coverage for an accident than the minimum limits established in the MCS-90.[265]

> **Pro Note:** The MCS-90 may permit recovery up to its stated amount, even when the insurer has available coverage defenses. "[A]ccording to the majority case law, the MCS-90 endorsement, its terms, and its operating provisions…supersede any limitation in the underlying insurance policy…as between an injured member of the public and the MCS-90 insurer."[266]

In lieu of an MCS-90 endorsement, the motor carrier may maintain a surety bond (Form MCS-82) in the same amount required by statute.[267] Or, the motor carrier may obtain authorization by the FMCSA to "self-insure." This requires a "satisfactory" safety rating.[268]

---

[260] <u>Carolina Cas. Ins. Co. v. Yeates</u>, 584 F.3d 868, 878 (10th Cir. 2009).
[261] <u>Id.</u>
[262] <u>Id.</u>
[263] <u>Canal Ins. Co. v. Carolina Cas. Ins. Co.</u>, 59 F.3d 281, 283 (1st Cir. 1995).
[264] <u>Campbell v. Bartlett</u>, 975 F.2d 1569, 1581 (10th Cir. 1992).
[265] <u>Hamm v. Canal Ins. Co.</u>, 10 F. Supp. 2d 539 (M.D.N.C. 1998) (the MCS-90 provides a limit *per accident*, as opposed to *per person*).
[266] <u>Id.</u>; <u>Cagle v. Wesco Ins. Co.</u>, No. 2:21-CV-52, 2021 U.S. Dist. LEXIS 253756, *9-10 (N.D. Ga. Dec. 6, 2021) (Story, R.).
[267] 49 C.F.R. § 387.7(d)(2).
[268] 49 C.F.R. § 387.7(d)(3).

4.16.2 Insurer's Duty to Defend Legal Actions

The FMCSR requirement of "financial responsibility" does not require an insurer to defend a legal action, which is outside the scope of coverage under the insurance policy. "[T]he MCS-90 leaves unaffected any provisions of the underlying insurance policy that do not impact the insurer's duty to compensate injured members of the public. An important distinction, however, is that, although the MCS-90 itself does not impose a duty to defend upon the insurer, neither does it negate any such duty of the insurer arising under the policy or state law."[269]

In summary, the MCS-90 means the insurer, as surety, must pay the judgment against the motor carrier resulting from tortious actions in operation, maintenance or use of motor vehicles even if not specifically listed on the policy.[270] But, the MCS-90 does not require the insurer to defend the case.

4.16.3 Records of Insurance Coverage

Financial responsibility information is considered public information, and registered motor carriers must make it available to the public for inspection.[271] As such, a discovery request to a motor carrier should include the relevant financial responsibility information. In Georgia, our state requires full disclosure of insurance information.[272] Therefore, our standard practice is to send a request pursuant to this statute. However, in the event that your State does not provide such recourse, a request may be made pursuant to 49 C.F.R. § 387.7(e). This statute requires "proof of financial responsibility... [to] be produced for review upon reasonable request by a member of the public."[273]

[269] T.H.E. Ins. Co. v. Larsen Intermodal Servs., 242 F.3d 667, 677 (5th Cir. 2001).
[270] Carolina Cas. Ins. Co., 584 F.3d at 878; Canal Ins. Co, 59 F.3d at 283.
[271] 49 C.F.R. § 387.7(e).
[272] O.C.G.A. § 33-3-28.
[273] Id.

5

WHAT ARE THE PARTS OF A COMMERCIAL VEHICLE ACCIDENT CASE?

Now that we understand the regulatory framework behind a truck accident case and the general responsibilities of a motor carrier and driver, this section of the book focuses on the preparation of a commercial vehicle case. When first presented with a potential case, there are three basic questions:

- *Who are the (potentially) responsible parties?* The driver and the motor carrier are the most obvious defendants in the majority of truck wreck cases. However, there are many more potentially responsible parties.

- *What was the culpable conduct?* Once the potentially responsible parties are ascertained, we need to address the causes of the accident. In many commercial vehicle cases, culpable conduct is a combination of the conduct of various potentially responsible parties.

- *What are the potential causes of action?* There may be one or more legal theories applicable to conduct giving rise to a collision.

The answers to these questions will guide the preparation of any successful commercial motor vehicle case. We address each of these important topics below.

5.1 Who Are the Potentially Responsible Parties?

In commercial truck accidents, there are often multiple individuals or entities that share responsibility for the harm caused in an accident. Of course, the facts of the accident will guide the analysis.

While there are too many potentially-implicated parties to name, the below list identifies many of the common parties: (a) professional driver; (b) motor carrier; (c) supervisors, managers, or involved superiors of the motor carrier; (d) shippers (freight owners); (e) brokers (freight forwarders); (f) cargo loaders; (g) truck maintenance personnel or companies; (h) truck part manufacturers; (k) insurance companies; and (l) intermodal providers.

5.1.1 Joint Tortfeasors in a Commercial Motor Vehicle Case

As in all tort cases, a tort case concerning a commercial motor vehicle accident may involve multiple joint tortfeasors. There is no Federal cause of action in such a case, so the state-law-based cause of action becomes relevant. We will focus on Georgia law for purposes of example.

Georgia law recognizes joint and several liability in instances where tortious conduct gives rise to joint liability. When the alleged negligent acts of two or more tortfeasors result in a single and indivisible injury, such as death, the alleged tortfeasors may be sued jointly.[274]

Styling a claim in a truck crash case is a strategic undertaking. For instance, bringing a tort suit against only a motor carrier may be advisable

---

[274] Id.

rather than bringing a claim against both the motor carrier and driver. Likewise, a suit against a motor carrier and the insurance carrier (where permitted by local law) may be the wise strategy. In addition, because there are multiple potentially culpable entities, it is important to lock the motor carrier into a position of identifying who (if any) additional persons they contend are liable, before the statute of limitation expires.

The point is, there are numerous strategic factors that affect the decision of who to sue. Let's start by looking at situations where suing the truck driver arises.

5.1.2 Truck Driver

The driver is a common defendant in commercial motor vehicle cases that result from driver acts or omissions. The FMCSR lay out standards for safety in the performance of a driver's primary responsibilities which could give rise to liability. A professional driver is subject to these regulations and, as such, may be liable under state law for violating the standard of conduct set forth in the Federal regulations.

> **Pro Note:** Use the Federal Motor Carrier Safety Regulations to form the basis of a negligence *per se* claim against the driver.

It is important to remember that the truck driver may be an agent/employee of a trucking company. The question will be: is the driver an independent contractor or an agent that the truck company maintains control over?[275] In addition, the truck driver may be a "dual agent" of more than one master.[276] This is a key inquiry, as it can, potentially, open up additional avenues of recovery. If the truck driver is the agent of two companies, then the potential for recovery has doubled.

---

[275] O.C.G.A. § 51-2-5(5).
[276] Enviromediation Servs., LLC v. Boatwright, 256 Ga. App. 200 (2002).

A plaintiff's attorney must make a strategic decision whether the driver is a necessary party and a wise addition to the case. The driver may be a sympathetic figure, depending on the facts and circumstances of the accident. However, the driver's addition may be necessary (at least at first) to ensure that there are no agency issues with the companies in question. It is ultimately a strategic question each attorney must address.

5.1.3 Commercial Motor Carrier (Trucking Company)

There are two common claims against the motor carrier in a truck crash case: (1) direct negligence and (2) imputed liability. In direct negligence, the motor carrier may be liable for its own actions in hiring, supervising, dispatching, aiding violation of Federal rules, and similar conduct. As detailed in section 4, *infra*, for example, the motor carrier has specific duties to fulfill when hiring a driver or maintaining the vehicle.[277] Where the failure to fulfill these duties is causally connected to the accident, a claim for violation of the motor carrier's duties under the FMCSR may add strategic value to the case.

Most commonly, however, the motor carrier faces potential "vicarious liability" based upon the theory of "*respondeat superior.*"[278] This creates liability for the motor carrier for the acts and omissions of an employee-driver within the course and scope of their employment, while operating the tractor-trailer.

Commercial motor vehicle practitioners must move a simple negligence claim to a professional negligence claim. This requires investigation into the operations of the commercial carrier to understand patterns and practices. If the motor carrier or driver has consistently violated the standards for professional drivers, then the facts of the case may be viewed in a different light by a judge or jury.

---

[277] 49 C.F.R. § 391.23 (hiring); 49 C.F.R. § 396 (maintenance).
[278] See, e.g., O.C.G.A § 51-2-2 (*respondeat superior* under Georgia law).

5.1.4 Shipper (Freight Owner)

Shippers face potential liability for harm caused to third parties by the cargo they are shipping or receiving. There are two main causes of action against a shipper. *One*, there may be a claim against the shipper for acts and omissions of the driver in the course and scope of the shipment.[279] *Two*, there may be a claim against the shipper for its *own* tortious acts and omissions which contribute to the collision.

To hold the shipper liable for the acts and omissions of the driver or motor carrier, the shipper must retain a requisite level of control over the delivery process.[280] This will be a fact-intensive inquiry, governed largely by the state law, and is akin to an independent contractor analysis.[281] For example, where the shipper paid the driver directly, imposed rules and fines for various acts/omissions in the course of shipment, required a particular type of equipment for shipment, and required pick-up and drop-off at a particular location, the shipper could be held liable for the acts and omissions of the driver.[282]

A shipper may also be liable for its own acts and omissions in the course of shipment. A shipper may be held liable, for example, for negligent hiring or "selection" of a motor carrier in the course of shipment.[283] Once again, this will be an inquiry governed by state law. For example, a Federal court in West Virginia held that under West Virginia law, "the shipper could be liable if its negligent selection of an incompetent independent contractor to do work which involves a risk of physical harm to others unless skillfully and carefully done was a proximate cause of the accident."[284] The Court held that the shipper had

---

[279] McLaine v. McLeod, 291 Ga. App. 335 (2008) (no liability for shipper because no control over shipment).
[280] Id.
[281] Sperl v. C.H. Robinson Worldwide, Inc., 946 N.E. 2d 463 (Ill. App. 2011) (a shipper is liable because it exercised a great deal of control over the shipment).
[282] Id.
[283] See, e.g., Jones v. CH Robinson Worldwide, 558 F.Supp.2d 630 (W.D. Va. 2008).
[284] Id. (internal citations omitted) (cleaned up).

a duty to investigate the motor carrier's "safety and fitness" to determine whether it was appropriate for handling the shipment.[285]

As previously discussed, the motor carrier and driver have a duty to ensure proper loading of shipments. However, when the shipper loads the goods, it may be responsible for the negligent loading.[286] This does not mean that the motor carrier is absolved of responsibility. If the motor carrier should have discovered the negligently loaded material, then it too may be held responsible.[287]

The FMCSR also impose duties upon the shipper when shipping hazardous materials.[288] This includes requirements that the hazardous material is properly marked, packaged, manufactured, and assembled.[289] A shipper's failure to satisfy all requirements may give rise to liability.

5.1.5 Cargo Loader

As detailed above, the FMCSR contain regulations specific to loading material. In certain situations, the loader of cargo bears responsibility for negligence in loading which contributes to a commercial motor vehicle collision.[290] The loader of cargo on a commercial vehicle may be any number of individuals, including the driver, employees of the trucking company, the shipping company, freight forwarder, or a third-party loading company.

The most common form of loading accident is when cargo is loaded inappropriately and shifts or falls causing injury to someone nearby. More specific examples include when a loader uses incorrect straps, overloads

---

[285] Id.

[286] "When the shipper assumes the responsibility of loading, the general rule is that he becomes liable for the defects which are latent and concealed and cannot be discerned by ordinary observation by the agents of the carrier...." U.S. v. Savage Truck Line, 209 F.2d. 442, 446 (4th Cir. 1953).

[287] Id.

[288] 49 C.F.R. § 173.22.

[289] Id.

[290] See, e.g., Savage Truck Line, 209 F.2d. at 446 (shipper liable for negligence in loading).

the trailer, or fails to use enough tie-downs. Remember that there are specific regulations regarding the number and types of tie-downs that must be used for loading certain materials.[291]

A common fact pattern in improper loading cases is a trailer is loaded improperly and, during travel, the load shifts causing the trailer to overturn or the cargo to fall. In this type of case, it is necessary to determine (a) the entity responsible for the loading; (b) the methods taken to load; and (c) the regulations that may apply.

5.1.6 Broker

A broker is a middle-man who connects a shipper (owner of goods) with a transportation company (motor carrier). As a middle-man between shippers and carriers, freight brokers play a vital role in the transportation industry. However, their involvement in the process of arranging transportation can also expose them to legal liability in the event of a truck accident.

Under Federal law, a "broker" is defined as "a person, other than a motor carrier or an employee or agent of a motor carrier, that as a principal or agent sells, offers for sale, negotiates for, or holds itself out by solicitation, advertisement, or otherwise as selling, providing, or arranging for, transportation by motor carrier for compensation."[292] While this may sound like a passive role, in recent years, courts have increasingly held freight brokers responsible for accidents involving commercial motor vehicles.

The theories are generally as follows. *One*, the broker "negligently hired" the motor carrier, leading to a motor carrier accepting a load when it was unfit. These claims face a challenging hurdle in preemption

---

[291] FMCA, Motor Carrier Safety Planner, https://csa.fmcsa.dot.gov/safetyplanner/MyFiles/SubSections.aspx?ch=22&sec=64&sub=132 (last accessed Mar. 3, 2023).
[292] 49 U.S.C. § 13102(2).

via Federal statute.[293] *Two*, the broker exercised such control over the shipment to create an agency relationship. These inquiries fall along the same lines as is an independent contractor or agent inquiry. That is, how much control was exercised by the broker over the motor carrier?[294]

5.1.7 Truck or Part Manufacturers

When a commercial motor vehicle accident occurs due to a defective product, such as faulty brakes or tires, a product liability case may be pursued against the manufacturer of the defective product. While the focus of this handbook is not product liability law, it is worth noting that the truck or part manufacturer is a potentially responsible party in litigation if a defective product contributes to an accident. This is because manufacturers have a legal duty to design and produce products that are reasonably safe for their intended use.[295] If they fail to do so and an injury or accident occurs as a result, they may be held liable for damages under product liability law.

We have handled cases in which a tire unexpectedly exploded, for example, causing serious bodily injury. The inquiry will follow the product liability standards of your jurisdiction.[296]

5.1.8 Maintenance Companies

As detailed above, the FMSCR require the motor carrier and the driver to undertake certain duties to ensure that the commercial motor vehicle is in working order. Motor carriers may outsource all or some of this responsibility to a third-party maintenance company. This is because the motor carrier may not have the ability to conduct significant repairs to the vehicle in-house.

---

[293] Ying Te v. Global Sunrise, Inc., 2020 U.S. Dist. LEXIS 37142, No. 1:18-CV-01961 (Mar. 4, 2020).

[294] Id.

[295] See, e.g., O.C.G.A. § 51-1-11 (Georgia law on product liability).

[296] Id.

When these repairs are negligently made, the maintenance company may be liable. The claim centers on whether or not the maintenance company exercised reasonable care in performing the repairs.[297]

When repairs are negligently completed, even by an outside party, the motor carrier may also be liable. In one case, for example, a motor carrier attempted to avoid liability for a rusted drag link which caused a collision. The motor carrier argued it could not be liable for the negligent maintenance because it outsourced all maintenance to a third-party. The court held that this outsourcing did not insulate the motor carrier from liability: "A reasonable jury could conclude that [the motor carrier] had a duty under the FMCSR to properly maintain and inspect the tractor/truck and that they have failed to do so."[298]

> **Pro Note:** A motor carrier may still be liable for improper maintenance, even when a third-party maintenance company negligently performed repairs which caused the accident.[299]

5.1.9 Insurance Company (or Companies)

Truck accidents often involve a complicated web of insurers. Each of the aforementioned potential defendants may have insurance coverage for the type of injuries or damages suffered in the vehicle accident. This insurance can be significant, as FMCSR require $750,000 or more in insurance in many instances.[300]

Unlike most other cases, in a commercial motor vehicle case, the Plaintiff can name the insurer as a party-defendant in some instances. The law that permits such a claim is known as a "direct action" statute.

---

[297] Byers v. Cent. Transp., LLC, 2019 U.S. Dist. LEXIS 85360, No. No. 19-cv-0107 (N.M.D.C. May 21, 2019).
[298] Esteras, 2006 U.S. Dist. LEXIS 60437 at *12.
[299] Id.
[300] See, Section 4.16, *supra*.

Georgia, for example, permits the insurer to be a named party. There are two direct action statutes in Georgia.

O.C.G.A. § 46-7-12(c) states, "[i]t shall be permissible under this article for any person having a cause of action arising under this article to join in the same action the motor carrier and the insurance carrier, whether arising in tort or contract." And O.C.G.A. § 40-2- 40(d)(4) states, "[a]ny person having a cause of action, whether arising in tort or contract, under this Code section may join in the same cause of action the motor carrier and its insurance carrier." Georgia law is clear that these statutes permit the addition of the insurer as a party defendant.[301] This can be a powerful tool to ensure coverage is afforded and the rights of the plaintiff are protected.

5.1.10 Intermodal Equipment Providers

"Intermodal shipping" concerns the shipment of freight containers by sea, rail, and truck. To understand intermodal shipping, the following definitions are relevant:

- *Intermodal equipment means trailing equipment that is used in the intermodal transportation of containers over public highways in interstate commerce, including trailers and chassis.*[302]

- *Intermodal equipment provider means any person that interchanges intermodal equipment with a motor carrier pursuant to a written interchange agreement or has a contractual responsibility for the maintenance of the intermodal equipment.*[303]

Some companies that serve as Intermodal Equipment Providers (IEP or IEPs) are ocean shipping companies, cargo ports, trucking companies,

---

[301] Jackson v. Sluder, 256 Ga. App. 812 (2002); Bramlett v. Bajric, 2012 U.S. Dist. LEXIS 148797 (N.D. Ga. Oct. 17, 2012).
[302] 49 C.F.R. § 390.5.
[303] 49 C.F.R. § 390.5.

and equipment leasing companies. IEPs are required to register with the FMCSA.[304] IEPs are subject to the same provisions of FMCSR as a motor carrier, except for the requirement to maintain an accident register.[305] One key consideration is the requirement that the chassis/trailers involved in the intermodal equipment transportation be properly maintained. The FMCSR require the IEPs to maintain, repair, and inspect the equipment.[306]

5.1.11 Claims Against Government for "Road Defects"

A government entity or third-party contractor may be liable for hazardous road conditions if those conditions contribute to a collision. This scenario most commonly occurs, in our experience, in work zone accidents. Other examples of hazards may include potholes, rubber from truck tire re-treads (commonly known as road gators), debris, lack of road lines or reflectors, absent or unmarked guard rails, low-hanging power lines, downed trees, lack of signage, and poorly maintained bridges. Claims against a state or local government will likely require a waiver of sovereign immunity, pursuant to State or Federal law.

In Georgia, O.C.G.A. § 32-2-2 requires the DOT to manage, construct, and maintain public highways.[307] This includes the "responsibility for all construction, maintenance, or any other work upon the state highway system."[308] These claims are usually presented pursuant to the Georgia Tort Claims Act.[309]

---

[304] 49 C.F.R. § 390.19.

[305] 49 C.F.R. § 385.503.

[306] 49 C.F.R. § 390.3(h).

[307] O.C.G.A. § 32-2-2.

[308] Jackson v. DOT, 201 Ga. App. 863, 864 (1991).

[309] O.C.G.A. § 50-21-20, et seq.

5.2 What Was the Culpable Conduct?

Now that we have identified the most likely potentially culpable parties, it is important to review the most common types of culpable conduct.

The types of activity giving rise to potential legal liability differs with each type of responsible party. Thus, the assessment of potentially culpable conduct must be made on a case-by-case basis. For example, manufacturer liability depends largely upon product design or manufacture.[310] Service providers, such as maintenance companies and cargo loaders, face liability when their conduct drops below a reasonable standard of care in performing services.[311]

This section will focus on the two most common categories of defendants (truck drivers and motor carriers) and the most commonly asserted violations by the same. There are multiple other potential responsible parties in a commercial motor vehicle case. If you have a claim against another category of entity, please contact us for more information on prosecuting the claim.

Generally, the commercial driver and motor carrier must comply with the requirements of the FMCSR, the applicable state Rules of the Road, and accepted standards of industry practice.[312] Failure to adhere to these standards are the basis for assessing potential liability of a responsible party. The claims that result will be negligence, negligence *per se*, recklessness, or intentionality, depending on the type of conduct at issue.

5.2.1 Commercial Driver and Carrier Liability

When we assess a commercial motor vehicle case, we begin with a checklist of potentially culpable conduct. We assess each aspect of the

---

[310] See, Section 5 above, *supra.*
[311] Id.
[312] See, Section 2.3, *supra.*

commercial vehicle case to determine the potential claims. Here is a checklist that we use:

We assess professional driver acts or omissions, including but not limited to the following:

- Lack of Driver Skill

- Distracted Driving

  ○ Cell Phone Use

  ○ Other Distractions

- Violation of Rules of the Road

- Deviation from Industry Standards

- Drowsy Driving and Hours of Service Rules

- Driver Impairment (Drugs or Alcohol)

- Failure to Maintain or Inspect Equipment

- Stopped Vehicles - Lighting and Warning

- Weather Hazards

We also assess motor carrier acts or omissions, including but not limited to the following:

- Driver Error and *Respondeat Superior*

- Improper Dispatching

- Negligent Hiring, Entrustment, or Retention

- Improper Cargo Loading

Each of these potentially culpable activities are covered in turn below. This is not an exhaustive list, of course. But, it is instead a list of commonly litigated issues in commercial motor vehicle cases in our experience.

5.2.2 Lack of Driver Skill

Like any other technical skill, it takes time to become proficient at driving a commercial vehicle. A fundamental element of most commercial motor vehicle cases is a claim that the driver failed to exercise the requisite level of skill at the time of the wreck.[313] In order to determine the standard of care required, a competent truck wreck attorney examines the following: (a) the FMCSR as applicable; (b) the State regulations as applicable; (c) industry standards put forth by the corporations involved and well known trainers, such as JJ Keller & Associates; and, (d) expert opinion.[314]

Examples of actions that fall below the standard of care may include swinging too wide or too narrow, running off of the road, failing to maintain lane, improper backing, or simply failing to follow the prescribed requirements of safe vehicle operations. Comparing those actions with the standard of care is a key *first step* to many truck accident cases.

5.2.3 Distracted Driving

A tractor-trailer may weigh as much as 80,000 pounds or more.[315] As a result, a truck takes 40% <u>longer</u> (than a civilian vehicle) to come to a complete stop when traveling 65mph on standard road conditions.[316] Likewise, a tractor-trailer takes up to 16 seconds to complete a left turn and clear an intersection.[317] Therefore, distracted driving can mean life and death.

---

[313] <u>Luxenburg v. Aycock</u>, 41 Ga. App. 722, 154 S.E. 460 (1930).
[314] See, Sec. 3, supra.
[315] Department of Transportation for Utah, Website, https://trucksmart.udot.utah.gov/stopping-distances/ (last accessed Apr. 25, 2023).
[316] <u>Id.</u>
[317] Schneider Transportation, Website, https://schneiderjobs.com/blog/turn-left-with-tractor-trailer (last accessed Apr. 25, 2023).

Distracted driving is the inability to show the requisite amount of attention to the road because something else is diverting the driver's attention. The sources of distraction are infinite.

> **Pro Note:** A human factors expert may be used to detail potential distractions while driving.[318] Some of the more commonly litigated distractions potentially affecting a driver, include the following: eating, listening to the radio, daydreaming, and conversation. In addition, in recent years, there has been increasing litigation on cell phone use as a potential distraction for professional drivers. A human factors expert may be engaged to opine that cell phone use was (or was not) a contributing factor to the collision.

The FMCSR specifically prohibit texting and driving.[319] The FMCSR also prohibit using a hand-held mobile device while driving.[320] Likewise, in Georgia, texting while driving or talking on the phone (without a handsfree device) is against the law for civilian motorists and commercial truckers.[321] Let's look at each of these provisions.

49 C.F.R. § 392.80 prohibits texting while driving. As it states clearly, "[n]o driver shall engage in texting while driving."[322] It also imposes a duty on the motor carrier. "No motor carrier shall allow or require its drivers to engage in texting while driving."[323]

49 C.F.R. § 392.82 also prohibits using a "hand-held mobile telephone" while driving.[324] "No driver shall use a hand-held mobile telephone while driving a CMV."[325] It also imposes a duty on the motor carrier. "No motor

---

[318] See, e.g., Ga. DOT v. Owens, 330 Ga. App. 123 (2014) (human factors expert testified that a dump truck created a hazard).
[319] 49 C.F.R. § 392.80.
[320] 49 C.F.R. § 392.82.
[321] O.C.G.A. § 40-6-241.2.
[322] 49 C.F.R. § 392.80(a).
[323] 49 C.F.R. § 392.80(b).
[324] 49 C.F.R. § 392.82(a).
[325] Id.

carrier shall allow or require its drivers to use a hand-held mobile telephone while driving a CMV."[326] Note that while it prohibits using a "hand-held" device, it does not apply to the use of a handsfree device.

The Georgia rules are similar. Georgia law expressly bars texting, in almost any manner, while driving. O.C.G.A. § 40-6-241.2 reads as follows: "No person who is 18 years of age or older or who has a Class C license shall operate a motor vehicle on any public road or highway of this state while using a wireless telecommunications device to write, send, or read any text based communication, including but not limited to a text message, instant message, e-mail, or Internet data."[327] There are, of course, exceptions for emergency reporting; but, for the most part, it is prohibited.

In addition, Georgia law expressly proscribes the use of a cellular phone, in almost any manner, while driving. O.C.G.A. § 40-6-241 prohibits anyone, including commercial drivers, from "physically hold[ing] or support[ing]" a phone with their body.[328] It also prohibits holding the phone for use in virtually anyway, including (a) navigation or (b) video streaming.[329] Commercial drivers are barred from using "more than a single button" to interact with a phone. Commercial drivers are also prohibited from "reach[ing]" for the phone in a manner that causes the driver to no longer be "in a seated driving position" or buckled.[330]

> **Pro Note:** While some cell phone use is permitted (like, for example, talking on the phone with a handsfree device), other industry standards may impose stricter limitations on commercial drivers. We have handled cases, for example, where the internal policies of the trucking company do not permit any cell phone use while driving.

---

[326] Id.
[327] O.C.G.A. § 40-6-241.2.
[328] O.C.G.A. § 40-6-241.
[329] Id.
[330] Id.

5.2.4 Negligence *Per Se*, Violation of "Rules of the Road"

In addition to the provisions of the FMCSR, state law applicable to traffic collisions may form a basis for liability. These "Rules of the Road" may provide additional, more stringent standards for the truck driver and motor carrier involved. The FMCSR do not preclude states from establishing standards for driver conduct within the state. Specifically, 49 C.F.R. § 390.9 states that the FMCSR are "not intended to preclude States or subdivisions thereof from establishing or enforcing State or local laws relating to safety, the compliance with which would not prevent full compliance with these regulations by the person subject thereto."[331] Because our law firm is based in Georgia, we will utilize the Georgia rules as a state-specific example of how the Rules of the Road can form the basis of a negligence *per se* claim.

Georgia establishes standards of road operations that commercial drivers and others must follow. All drivers in Georgia, commercial and civilian, are required to adhere to the "Uniform Rules of the Road." These statutory rules can be found at O.C.G.A. § 40-6-1 through 40-6-397.

> **Pro Note:** Georgia has adopted the FMCSR as the standard for operations of intrastate carriers as well.[332]

The Georgia "Uniform Rules of the Road" govern many areas of safety such as:

* obeying the instructions of a mechanical traffic control device (O.C.G.A. § 40-6-20 through 40-6-26);

* passing or overtaking other vehicles (O.C.G.A. § 40-6-40 through 40-6-46);

* following too closely (O.C.G.A. § 40-6-49);

---

[331] 49 C.F.R. § 390.9.
[332] Ga. Comp. R. & Regs. 515-16-4-.01.

- making proper right or left hand turns within intersections (O.C.G.A. § 40-6-70 through 40-6-71; 40-6-120 through 40-6-126);

- obeying stop signs and yield signs (O.C.G.A. § 40-6-72);

- obeying posted speed limits and driving at appropriate rates of speed (O.C.G.A. § 40-6-180 through 40-6-188); and

- driving while intoxicated (O.C.G.A. § 40-6-391 through 40-6-392).

The Uniform Rules of the Road of any state must be considered carefully when evaluating a truck accident case.

5.2.5 Deviation from Industry Standards

Commercial motor carriers also have industry standards with which they must comply. The motor carrier's own internal standards and industry-recognized-leaders in motor carrier compliance are two significant sources of information concerning the standard of care. "Training materials for professional truck drivers are relevant to this case as evidence of what an ordinarily prudent person engaged as a professional truck driver would have done when confronted with the same circumstances."[333]

In addition to internal training materials, there are companies that specialize in training drivers. One of the best known is JJ Keller, a company that specializes in education and training of truck drivers. The materials published by companies like JJ Keller may be reviewed and compared to your commercial motor vehicle collision.[334]

---

[333] Glass v. Mecham, 2014 U.S. Dist. LEXIS 192653 (W.D. Okl. Jul. 7, 2014).
[334] JJ Keller's Website, https://www.jjkeller.com/ (last accessed Jan, 11, 2023).

> **Pro Note:** While training materials may inform the standard of care, there is generally no Federal requirement for a motor carrier to train their drivers. "The Federal Motor Carrier Safety Regulations generally do not require trucking companies to train their drivers. For instance, when a driver has a valid CDL, the motor carrier may accept the CDL in lieu of subjecting the driver to a road test."[335]

We have previously used experts in truck accident regulations with success. Competent experts may opine as to the standard of care for professional drivers, when it is outside the knowledge of the average juror.[336]

5.3 Drowsy Driving and Hours of Service Rules

A sleepy truck driver is bad news. The FMCSA knows this, and they have issued regulations to govern the hours a truck driver may operate a vehicle. Familiarity with the rules governing hours of service is critical for any case in which sleepiness or drowsiness is thought to be a factor.

5.3.1 Hours of Service Rules

A truck driver is subject to specific rules that control the number of hours that he or she can operate the truck ("on-duty time") and how many hours of rest between shifts ("non-operating hours"). These rules control the maximum number of hours a truck driver can operate the truck in a single day, as well as the maximum number of hours in a week. The rules can be confusing, absent significant work.[337]

---

[335] Ortiz v. Wiwi, 2012 U.S. Dist. LEXIS 137881 at *12 (M.D. Ga. 2012).
[336] Castle-Foster v. Cintas Corp., 2021 US. Dist. LEXIS 28145 (S.D. Ga. Feb. 16, 2021) (permitting an expert to testify on the standards for professional drivers because it is "beyond the knowledge of a layperson.").
[337] 49 C.F.R. § 395.

To facilitate an understanding of these rules, we will discuss the definition of "on duty time" and "non-operating hours." Then, we will turn to the property carrying rules, followed by the passenger carrying rules.

5.3.2 Definition of On-Duty Time and Non-Operating Hours

One important regulation to be familiar with is 49 C.F.R. § 395.2, which outlines the definition of "on-duty hours" for commercial motor vehicle drivers. According to the code section, "on-duty" time means "all time from the time a driver begins to work or is required to be in readiness to work until the time the driver is relieved from work and all responsibility for performing work."[338]

The definition expressly lists a number of activities in the definition of on-duty time. This includes time spent waiting to be dispatched at a plant, terminal, or other property of a motor carrier or shipper, as well as time spent inspecting, servicing, or conditioning a commercial motor vehicle.[339] Additionally, any time spent in a commercial motor vehicle is on-duty, except (i) resting in a parked vehicle, (ii) resting in a sleeper berth, or (iii) riding in the passenger seat for up to 3 hours.[340]

Other activities that fall under on-duty time include (i) loading or unloading a commercial motor vehicle, (ii) supervising or assisting in the loading or unloading a commercial vehicle, (iii) obtaining assistance for a disabled vehicle, (iv) providing a breath or urine sample, or (v) performing any other work for a motor carrier or non-motor carrier for compensation. This last category is critical as it can encompass a second job, unrelated to driving a commercial motor vehicle.[341]

---

[338] 49 C.F.R. § 395.2.
[339] 49 C.F.R. § 395.2(1)(2).
[340] 49 C.F.R. § 395.2(4).
[341] 49 C.F.R. § 395.2(5)-(9).

Obviously, all "driving time" is also included in on-duty time.[342] It is important to note, however, that on-duty time is <u>not</u> the same as driving time for purposes of the hours of service rules.

5.3.3 Hours of Service Rules for Property Carrying

The general rules for property-carrying tractor trailers are as follows. As an initial matter, there is a 14-hour driving-window limit. This means a driver is permitted a period of 14 consecutive hours in which to drive his vehicle. This does not mean the driver can operate the vehicle this whole time. Once that period expires, the driver is required to take 10 consecutive hours off before driving again.[343]

Within this 14-hour driving window, the truck driver may operate the truck for 11 hours. A rest break of 30 consecutive minutes is required after 8 hours of driving. This could be a food or rest break, or another time when the driver is not driving.[344]

In addition to daily limits, a truck driver has a weekly limit for hours of service. The weekly limit is commonly referred to as the 60/70-hour rule. The driver is permitted to be "on duty" 60 hours per 7 days, if the trucking company operates 6 days a week. If the trucking company operates 7 days a week, the driver is permitted to be "on duty" 70 hours per 8-day period. This is sometimes referred to as a "weekly" limit. Importantly, however, the 7-8-day period does not have to begin at the start of the week. It refers to the days immediately prior to the current day.[345]

Here is an example to bring the 60/70-hour rule home. Let's assume a driver has the following hours:

---

[342] 49 C.F.R. § 395.2(3).
[343] 49 C.F.R. § 395.3(a)(2).
[344] 49 C.F.R. § 395.3(a)(3).
[345] 49 C.F.R. § 395.3(b).

DAY	HOURS
1. Sunday	0
2. Monday	10
3. Tuesday	8.5
4. Wednesday	12.5
5. Thursday	9
6. Friday	10
7. Saturday	12
8. Sunday	5
TOTAL	67 hours

In this scenario, if the truck company operates <u>six</u> days per week, then the truck driver is <u>over</u> hours and legally unable to drive on Sunday. If, however, the truck company operates <u>seven</u> days per week, the truck driver is <u>not</u> over hours on Sunday. But, the truck driver only has 3 hours available for the next Monday. Charting the hours out is key to understanding the hours of service as applicable to a driver.

A driver may re-set their "weekly" (60/70) hour limit with a 34-hour reset. "Any period of 7 [or 8] consecutive days may end with the beginning of an off-duty period of 34 or more consecutive hours."[346] The general rules for passenger-carrying commercial motor vehicles are discussed below.

5.3.4 Hours of Service Rules for Passenger Carrying

The hours-of-service rules for passenger carrying vehicles generally follow the same parameters as the property carrying rules (daily and weekly on-duty and/or driving limits). As an initial matter, a driver has 15 hours of on-duty time, following 8 consecutive hours of off-duty time.[347] This does not mean the driver can operate the commercial vehicle for this entire time. Instead, the driver is limited to 10 hours of driving during this on-duty time.[348]

---

[346] 49 C.F.R. § 395.3(c).
[347] 49 C.F.R. §395.5(a)(2).
[348] 49 C.F.R. §395.5(a)(1).

The Federal Regulations also limit the weekly hours. Just like property carrying vehicles, there is a 60/70 hour "weekly" limit. This means that if the passenger-carrying motor carrier operates 6 days per week, then there is an on-duty limit of "60 hours in any 7 consecutive days."[349] If the passenger-carrying motor carrier operates 7 days per week, then there is a limit for "on duty" of "70 hours in any 8 consecutive days."[350]

5.3.5 Some Common Exceptions

There are a number of exceptions to the hours of service rules in the C.F.R. and each should be studied carefully. We will address three of the most commonly litigated exceptions below.

5.3.5.A Air-Mile Exception

There is a common exception referred to as the "100 air-mile exception." The 100 air-mile exception exempts a driver from the log-book reporting requirements, as well as the 30-minute-break requirement. To qualify for the exception, the driver must operate within a "100 air-mile radius" of his normal work-reporting location. The driver must return to this work reporting location within 12 hours. The driver is still subject to the 10-hour-off duty requirement and 11-hour driving limitation.[351]

There is also a 100-air mile exception for retail store deliveries, during the holiday seasons. The FMCSR exempt drivers on such routes from the daily and weekly limits as follows:

The provisions of § 395.3 (a) and (b) shall not apply with respect to drivers of commercial motor vehicles engaged solely in making local deliveries from retail stores and/or retail catalog businesses

---

[349] 49 C.F.R. § 395.5(b).
[350] Id.
[351] Id.

to the ultimate consumer, when driving solely within a 100-air mile radius of the driver's work-reporting location, during the period from December 10 to December 25, both inclusive, of each year.[352]

5.3.5.B Short Haul Exception

There is the 16-hour, short-haul exception for a property-carrying motor carrier. This exception allows a truck driver to extend the 14-hour driving window to 16 hours once every 7 days.[353] For this extension to apply, the driver must: (a) leave and return to the same reporting location each day and for the previous 5 days; (b) be off duty 10 consecutive hours each day; (c) be released from work within 16 hours of duty; and (d) not have used this exception more than once within their 60/70-hour weekly limit.[354] We often see this exception applied to local delivery drivers running routes throughout a community.

5.3.5.C Adverse Driving Condition Exception

There is an exception for "Adverse Driving Conditions." To complete a run in the event of unexpected, adverse conditions, the truck driver may drive an additional 2 hours during the 14-hour period outlined above. The conditions must (a) occur during the original 14-hour period and (b) be unexpected at the beginning of the run.[355]

> **Pro Note:** Both elements of the adverse driving exception must be met for it to apply. It is key that the condition that caused the delay be <u>unexpected</u> at the start of the route.

---

[352] 49 C.F.R. § 395.1(f).
[353] 49 C.F.R. § 395.1(o).
[354] Id.
[355] 49 C.F.R. § 395.1(b).

5.3.6 Motor Carrier Responsibilities

It is important to note that the motor carrier is not a passive observer of the hours-of-service rules. The FMCSR require that the motor carrier take an active part in requiring observance.

> *Whenever ... a duty is prescribed for a driver or a prohibition is imposed upon the driver, it shall be the duty of the motor carrier to require observance of such duty or prohibition. If the motor carrier is a driver, the driver shall likewise be bound.*[356]

Specifically, the Federal Regulations forbid the motor carrier from using a driver that is over hours. "[N]o motor carrier shall permit or require any driver used by it to drive a property-carrying commercial motor vehicle."[357] This applies to passenger carrying vehicles as well.[358]

In addition, the motor carrier must ensure the truck driver completes proper paperwork to track his/her hours of service. This is known as keeping a "driver log." The driver log is discussed further below. "Except for a private motor carrier of passengers (non-business)..., every motor carrier shall require every driver used by the motor carrier to record his/her duty status for each 24-hour period...."[359]

The takeaway from this section is that the motor carrier must have a system in place to monitor a driver's on-duty hours. For practical purposes, the motor carrier likely employs an electronic driver log system to keep track of these rules. If the motor carrier does not have such a system in place, it begs the question as to whether the carrier is meeting its obligations under the FMCSR.

---

[356] 49 C.F.R. § 390.11.
[357] 49 C.F.R. § 395.3(a).
[358] 49 C.F.R. § 395.5(a).
[359] 49 C.F.R. § 395.8.

5.3.7 Driver Logs

Federal law requires that commercial drivers maintain logs for their hours of service. This can be in the form of a written log or, more commonly, an electronic log that is maintained by a device in the motor vehicle. As of December 18, 2017, a motor carrier is required to "install and require" each its drivers to use an electronic log-tracking device ("ELD") in its tractors.[360] While ELDs are the standard, there are certain exceptions that permit written logs for a driver.[361] Therefore, we discuss those logs as well.

The logs will generally have four rows: "off duty," "sleeper berth," "driving," and "on-duty not driving."[362] On the bottom of the rows, it will have time for the hours. A line will then run from left-to-right, and up-and-down, to signify the hours of service. The logs will also include the following information: "(1) Date; (2) Total miles driving today; (3) Truck or tractor and trailer number; (4) Name of carrier; (5) Driver's signature/certification; (6) 24-hour period starting time (e.g. midnight, 9:00 a.m., noon, 3:00 p.m.); (7) Main office address; (8) Remarks; (9) Name of co-driver; (10) Total hours (far right edge of grid); (11) Shipping document number(s), or name of shipper and commodity."[363]

An example of a written log is listed below.

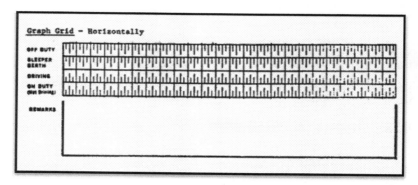

---

[360] 49 C.F.R. § 395.8(a)(1).
[361] Id.
[362] 49 C.F.R. § 395.8(b).
[363] 49 C.F.R. § 395.8(d).

The electronic logs appear like this.

Studying the logs is key to any case where drowsiness or sleepiness are issues.

5.3.8 Record Retention

49 C.F.R. § 395.8 provides the specific requirements for a driver to record his/her duty status.[364] This creates a volume of material that must be managed by the motor carrier. Depending on the size of the motor carrier, this may be tens of thousands of logs per day. The FMCSR require the motor carriers to maintain these records "for a period of not less than 6 months from the date of receipt."[365] The driver must also retain a copy of their record of duty status "for the previous 7 consecutive days which shall be in his/her possession and available for inspection while on duty."[366]

> **Pro Note:** A wise attorney pushes for the driver logs in any case in which driver drowsiness is suspected. If the driver or the motor carrier did not comply with the hours of service log requirements, including retention, this can be a game-changer if the facts show it is relevant.

Because the time period for retention of these records is limited, it is key to send a preservation demand for these records. A good preservation demand specifically states the obligations of both the carrier and driver.

---

[364] 49 C.F.R. § 395.8.
[365] 49 C.F.R. § 395.8(k)(1).
[366] 49 C.F.R. § 395.8(k)(2).

5.4 Drugs, Alcohol, and Driver Impairment

There are numerous Federal and state standards that limit the driver's operation of a vehicle when in an impaired condition or when the driver otherwise lacks the necessary alertness. Hindered ability or lack of alertness is commonly related to fatigue, illness, or other causes (such as drugs or alcohol). 49 C.F.R. § 392.3 prohibits driving while drowsy or otherwise not in an alert condition, as follows.

> No driver shall operate a commercial motor vehicle, and a motor carrier shall not require or permit a driver to operate a commercial motor vehicle, while the driver's ability or alertness is so impaired, or so likely to become impaired, through fatigue, illness, or any other cause, as to make it unsafe for him/her to begin or continue to operate the commercial motor vehicle.[367]

There is a limited exception, if there is a grave emergency which requires it.[368]

There is another subsection of the C.F.R. that deals specifically with drugs and alcohol. "No driver shall be on duty and possess, be under the influence of, or use, any of the following drugs or other substance...."[369] The specific drugs are discussed in the subsection below.

5.4.1 Intoxication (Drugs & Alcohol)

The Federal Regulations specifically prohibit any form of alcohol and drug use while operating a commercial vehicle. Specifically, in regard to drugs, it states the following:

> No driver shall be on duty and possess, be under the influence of, or use, any of the following drugs or other substances: (1) Any 21

[367] 49 C.F.R. § 392.3.
[368] Id.
[369] 49 C.F.R. § 392.4(a).

C.F.R. § 1308.11 Schedule I substance; (2) An amphetamine or any formulation thereof (including, but not limited, to "pep pills," and "bennies"); (3) A narcotic drug or any derivative thereof; or (4) Any other substance, to a degree which renders the driver incapable of safely operating a motor vehicle.[370]

In regard to alcohol use, the Federal Rules prohibit the use of alcohol within 4 hours of going on duty. The rules also prohibit being under "the influence of alcohol, or have any measured alcohol concentration, or detected presence of alcohol." The Federal Regulations further state that the driver should not possess alcoholic beverages in excess of 3-percent alcohol by volume.[371]

State law should also be considered, as the Federal law sets forth only the minimum standards. In Georgia, for example, it is illegal to be under the influence of alcohol or drugs if it makes the driver "less safe to drive."[372]

5.4.2 Safety-Sensitive Functions

When we traditionally think of impairment, we think of operating the motor vehicle. The Federal rules go further to limit driver activity by prohibiting a driver from taking part in any safety-sensitive function while under the influence of drugs or alcohol. In general, "no driver shall perform safety-sensitive functions, including driving a commercial motor vehicle" when they are under the influence of alcohol or controlled substances in violation of the Federal regulations.[373]

A safety sensitive function is defined broadly and, in general, encompasses all on-duty activities.[374] It includes equipment inspection,

---

[370] Id.
[371] 49 C.F.R. § 392.5.
[372] O.C.G.A. § 40-6-391(a).
[373] 49 C.F.R. § 382.501.
[374] 49 C.F.R. § 382.107.

all time driving (of course), time in the sleeper berth, all time unloading, loading, or supervising, and all time repairing the vehicle.[375] In our experience, the company standards will likely go further to require no drug or alcohol use when on-duty or within 4 hours of the same.

5.4.3 Drug and Alcohol Testing of Drivers

The FMCSR require motor carriers to test their truck drivers for drugs and alcohol in three scenarios. These include: (1) an initial employment test; (2) an after-the-accident test; and (3) random tests. We discuss each of these in turn below.

5.4.3.A Initial Employment Drug Test

A truck driver must take a drug test at the time of his initial employment. "Prior to the first time a driver performs safety-sensitive functions for an employer, the driver shall undergo testing for controlled substances as a condition prior to being used, unless the employer uses the exception in paragraph (b) of this section."[376] The exception to pre-employment screening applies if the driver was (a) participating in a controlled substances testing program within the prior 30 days; (b) was either tested in the prior 6 months or subject to random testing for the prior 12 months; and (c) the employer ensures that no prior employer has notice of a failed test in the last six months.[377]

DOT drug tests require testing for the following drugs: (a) Cocaine; (b) Phencyclidine (PCP); (c) Marijuana; (d) Methamphetamines and Amphetamines; and (e) Opiates.[378] These records must be kept for a designated period of time (discussed below).

---

[375] Id.
[376] 49 C.F.R. § 382.301.
[377] Id.
[378] 49 C.F.R. § 40.85.

5.4.3.B Drug Testing After an Accident

When the accident involves certain facts, the truck driver must receive a drug and alcohol test. A truck driver does <u>not</u> have to receive a screening just because he was involved in an accident.[379] Instead, the accident must meet certain requirements.

This chart is helpful for determining when a drug and alcohol test will be required:

Type of Accident Involved	Citation Issued to the CMV Driver	Test Must Be Performed by Employer
Human Fatality	Yes	Yes
Human Fatality	No	Yes
Bodily Injury with Immediate Medical Treatment Away from the Scene	Yes	Yes
Bodily Injury with Immediate Medical Treatment Away from the Scene	No	No
Disabling Damage to Any Motor Vehicle Requiring Tow Away	Yes	Yes
Disabling Damage to Any Motor Vehicle Requiring Tow Away	No	No

The essential rules are as follows: A drug/alcohol test is required (a) if there is a human fatality, (b) if the driver receives a citation *and* a person is taken from the scene for emergency medical treatment, <u>*or*</u> (c) if the driver receives a citation *and* a vehicle has disabling damage requiring a tow truck.[380]

---

[379] 49 C.F.R. § 382.303.
[380] <u>Id.</u>

5.4.3.C Random Drug and Alcohol Testing

The FMCSR require truck drivers to submit to random alcohol and drug tests. The percentage of truck drivers that a company must test is subject to change each year. In the original code section, it was 10% of drivers tested for alcohol in a year and 25% for drug tests within a year.[381] There are other less-common scenarios when a truck driver may be required to submit to a drug or alcohol test. These include when there exists reasonable suspicion of a drug/alcohol policy violation, and after a truck driver has failed or refused a test.[382]

5.4.3.D A Negative Test Is Required Before Returning to Work

If a commercial driver tests positive for drugs/alcohol in violation of policy or regulation, the motor carrier must do more than simply require the driver to wait a period of time before resuming operation of a motor vehicle. The Federal Regulations require a negative test before permitting that driver to return to work.[383] In our experience, many companies will have a higher standard in place such as a no-tolerance, internal policy for drug and alcohol use.

5.4.3.E Retention of Drug and Alcohol Testing Records

If drug and alcohol use is a potential issue in your case, then it is important to request the results of alcohol or drug tests. As detailed above, the FMCSR require the motor carrier to conduct random testing. The results from this program must also be maintained.[384]

Motor carriers bear the responsibility of maintaining test results in a secure and confidential manner. As such, you can request this information when relevant.

---

[381] 49 C.F.R. § 382.305.
[382] FMCSA Website, https://www.fmcsa.dot.gov/regulations/drug-alcohol-testing/what-tests-are-required-and-when-does-testing-occur (last accessed Apr. 27, 2023).
[383] 49 C.F.R. 382.309.
[384] 49 C.F.R. § 382.403(a).

The testing officer is required to maintain drug and alcohol tests for any negative drug and alcohol test for a period of one year.[385] A positive drug or alcohol test is required to be kept for three years.[386] The rules here interact in interesting ways. As you may recall from an earlier section, motor carriers are required to investigate the history of drivers, including requesting positive drug/alcohol tests from prior DOT employers.[387] Therefore, the motor carrier may have records on this subject above and beyond the time for which they employed the driver.

There are other records that a motor carrier is required to maintain. These include the following:

> *(i) A verified positive, adulterated, or substituted drug test result;*
>
> *(ii) An alcohol confirmation test with a concentration of 0.04 or higher;*
>
> *(iii) A refusal to submit to any test required by subpart C of this part;*
>
> *(iv) An employer's report of actual knowledge, as defined at § 382.107:*
>
> > *(A) On duty alcohol use pursuant to § 382.205;*
> >
> > *(B) Pre-duty alcohol use pursuant to § 382.207;*
> >
> > *(C) Alcohol use following an accident pursuant to § 382.209; and*
> >
> > *(D) Controlled substance use pursuant to § 382.213;*
>
> *(v) A substance abuse professional (SAP as defined in § 40.3 of this title) report of the successful completion of the return-to-duty process;*

---

[385] 49 C.F.R. § 382.409(a).
[386] Id.
[387] 49 C.F.R. § 382.413(a).

(vi) A negative return-to-duty test; and

(vii) An employer's report of completion of follow-up testing.[388]

5.4.4 Inspection, Repair, and Maintenance of Commercial Motor Vehicles

Too often, motor vehicle collisions are caused by the failure of equipment (such as brakes or steering systems). The FMCSR require equipment to be in good working order. This standard applies to parts and accessories as well. "Parts and accessories shall be in safe and proper operating condition at all times."[389] This regulation is applicable to any "parts and accessories which may affect safety of operation...."[390]

To facilitate this, the regulations require inspection, repair, and maintenance of equipment used in commercial transportation.[391] "Every motor carrier and intermodal equipment provider must systematically inspect, repair, and maintain, or cause to be systematically inspected, repaired, and maintained, all motor vehicles and intermodal equipment subject to its control."[392]

There are a variety of rules that govern inspection, repair, and maintenance of specific pieces of equipment. The assorted provisions are too numerous to state here, but a review of the table of contents of 49 C.F.R. § 393 is a good overview.

- Subpart A - General (§§ 393.1 - 393.7)

- Subpart B - Lamps, Reflective Devices, and Electrical Wiring (§§ 393.9 - 393.31-393.33)

- Subpart C - Brakes (§§ 393.40 - 393.55)

---

[388] 49 C.F.R. § 382.601(b)(12).
[389] Id.
[390] Id.
[391] 49 C.F.R. § 396.3(a)(1).
[392] Id.

- Subpart D - Glazing and Window Construction (§§ 393.60 - 393.63)

- Subpart E - Fuel Systems (§§ 393.65 - 393.69)

- Subpart F - Coupling Devices and Towing Methods (§§ 393.70 - 393.71)

- Subpart G - Miscellaneous Parts and Accessories (§§ 393.75 - 393.94)

- Subpart H - Emergency Equipment (§ 393.95)

- Subpart I - Protection Against Shifting and Falling Cargo (§§ 393.100 - 393.136)

- Subpart J - Frames, Cab and Body Components, Wheels, Steering, and Suspension Systems (§§ 393.201 - 393.209)

There are two key inspection requirements of which you should be aware. These include a yearly "DOT inspection" and daily inspections by the driver. The records of these inspections must be maintained for 18 months.[393] These are discussed below.

5.4.4.A Annual Inspections

FMCSR require the motor carrier to conduct annual inspections.[394] These inspections must be carried out by someone who is familiar with the requirements of Part 393, which are outlined above.[395] The annual inspection requires a detailed check (and repair) of all portions of the commercial motor vehicle.

Here is a checklist supplied by the FMCSA for completing the annual inspection. As you can see, the annual review requires a review of the (a) brake system; (b) coupling devices; (c) exhaust system; (d) fuel system; (e)

---

[393] 49 C.F.R. § 396.3(c).
[394] 49 C.F.R. § 396.17(d).
[395] 49 C.F.R. § 396.19.

lighting devices; (f) safe loading; (g) steering mechanism; (h) suspension; (i) frame; (j) tires; (k) wheels and rims; and (l) windshield.[396]

ANNUAL VEHICLE INSPECTION REPORT

	VEHICLE HISTORY RECORD	
	SIGNS	FLEET UNIT NUMBER
	DATE	

MOTOR CARRIER OPERATOR	INSPECTOR'S NAME (PRINT OR TYPE)
ADDRESS	THIS INSPECTOR MEETS THE QUALIFICATION REQUIREMENTS IN SECTION 396.19. ☐ YES
CITY, STATE, ZIP CODE	VEHICLE IDENTIFICATION [✓] AND COMPLETE: ☐ LIC. PLATE NO. ☐ VIN ☐ OTHER
VEHICLE TYPE ☐ TRACTOR ☐ TRAILER ☐ TRUCK ☐ (OTHER)	INSPECTION AGENCY/LOCATION (OPTIONAL)

VEHICLE COMPONENTS INSPECTED

OK	NEEDS REPAIR	REPAIRED	ITEM	OK	NEEDS REPAIR	REPAIRED	ITEM	OK	NEEDS REPAIR	REPAIRED	ITEM
			1. BRAKE SYSTEM				**4. FUEL SYSTEM**				**9. FRAME**
			a. Service Brakes				a. Visible leak				a. Frame Members
			b. Parking Brake System				b. Fuel tank filler cap missing				b. Tire and Wheel Clearance
			c. Brake Drums or Rotors				c. Fuel tank securely				c. Adjustable Axle
			d. Brake Hose				attached				Assemblies (Sliding
			e. Brake Tubing				**5. LIGHTING DEVICES**				Subframes)
			f. Low Pressure Warning				All lighting devices and				**10. TIRES**
			Device				reflectors required by Section				a. Tires on any steering axle
			g. Tractor Protection Valve				393 shall be operable.				of a power unit.
			h. Air Compressor				**6. SAFE LOADING**				b. All other tires.
			i. Electric Brakes				a. Part(s) of vehicle or				**11. WHEELS AND RIMS**
			j. Hydraulic Brakes				condition of loading such				a. Lock or Side Ring
			k. Vacuum Systems				that the spare tire or any				b. Wheels and Rims
							part of the load or dunnage				c. Fasteners
			2. COUPLING DEVICES				can fall onto the roadway.				d. Welds
			a. Fifth Wheels				b. Protection against shifting				**12. WINDSHIELD GLAZING**
			b. Pintle Hooks				cargo				Requirements and exceptions
			c. Drawbar/Towbar Eye				**7. STEERING MECHANISM**				as stated pertaining to any
			d. Drawbar/Towbar Tongue				a. Steering Wheel Free Play				crack, discoloration or vision
			e. Safety Devices				b. Steering Column				reducing matter (reference
			f. Saddle-Mounts				c. Front Axle Beam and All				393.60 for exceptions)
							Steering Components				**13. WINDSHIELD WIPERS**
			3. EXHAUST SYSTEM				Other Than Steering				Any power unit that has an
			a. Any exhaust system				Column				inoperative wiper, or missing
			determined to be leaking at				d. Steering Gear Box				or damaged parts that render
			a point forward of or directly				e. Pitman Arm				it ineffective.
			below the driver/sleeper				f. Power Steering				List any other condition which may
			compartment.				g. Ball and Socket Joints				prevent safe operation of this
			b. A bus exhaust system				h. Tie Rods and Drag Links				vehicle.
			leaking or discharging to				i. Nuts				
			the atmosphere in violation				j. Steering System				
			of standards (1), (2) or (3).				**8. SUSPENSION**				
			c. No part of the exhaust				a. Any U-bolt(s), spring				
			system of any motor vehicle				hanger(s), or other axle				
			shall be so located as				positioning part(s) cracked,				
			would be likely to result in				broken, loose or missing				
			burning, charring, or				resulting in shifting of an				
			damaging the electrical				axle from its normal position.				
			wiring, the fuel supply, or				b. Spring Assembly				
			any combustible part of the				c. Torque, Radius or Tracking				
			motor vehicle.				Components.				

INSTRUCTIONS: MARK COLUMN ENTRIES TO VERIFY INSPECTION: __X__ OK, __X__ NEEDS REPAIR, __NA__ IF ITEMS DO NOT APPLY, _____ REPAIRED DATE

CERTIFICATION: THIS VEHICLE HAS PASSED ALL THE INSPECTION ITEMS FOR THE ANNUAL VEHICLE INSPECTION REPORT IN ACCORDANCE WITH 49 CFR 396.

© Copyright 1994 & Published by J. J. KELLER & ASSOCIATES, INC.• Neenah, WI 54957-0368
PRINTED IN THE U.S.A.

280-F5-C3
Rev. 3/94

ORIGINAL

---

[396] FMCSA Website, https://www.fmcsa.dot.gov/sites/fmcsa.dot.gov/files/docs/part-396form6.pdf (last accessed Apr. 27, 2023).

5.4.4.B Daily Inspections

For many years, commercial drivers were required to perform pre-trip and post-trip inspections before and after every trip. This changed in a recent update to the FMCSR. As of the writing of this Manual, a driver does not have to do an inspection report before driving. Instead, the driver must "[b]e satisfied that the motor vehicle is in safe operating condition."[397] The driver only has to "[r]eview the last driver vehicle inspection report if required by § 396.11(a)(2)(ii)."[398] This section states that "[d]rivers are not required to prepare a report if no defect or deficiency is discovered by or reported to the driver." [399]

Given the longstanding requirement that predated this rule change, some motor carriers still require a pre-trip and post-trip inspection reports. These inspections are cursory in nature and generally include the following:

* Service brakes including trailer brake connections;
* Parking brake;
* Steering mechanism;
* Lighting devices and reflectors;
* Tires;
* Horn;
* Windshield wipers;
* Rear vision mirrors;
* Coupling devices;
* Wheels and rims; and
* Emergency equipment.[400]

Often records relating to such inspections are stored electronically. Whether physical or electronic, the records are only required to be maintained for three months.[401]

---

[397] 49 C.F.R. § 396.13(a).
[398] 49 C.F.R. § 396.11(a)(2)(i).
[399] Id.
[400] 49 C.F.R. § 396.11(a)(1).
[401] 49 C.F.R. § 396.11(a)(4).

5.5 Stopped Vehicles, Lighting and Warning

We have all seen a tractor-trailer stopped on the side of the road. This can be a highly dangerous situation. A large portion of the shoulder is overtaken. Sometimes a portion of the roadway is overtaken. There is a major risk of rear-ends and swerving accidents, when a tractor-trailer is stopped on the side of the road improperly. For this reason, the FMCSR require specific procedures for alerting others when stopping the vehicle in or alongside the highway.

49 C.F.R. § 392.8 and 392.22-33 establish rules for the use of emergency lighting and reflective equipment. "Whenever a commercial vehicle is stopped upon the traveled portion of a highway or the shoulder of a highway, the driver of the stopped vehicle shall immediately activate the hazard warning flashers and continue the flashing until the driver places warning devices next to the unit."[402]

After turning on the warning hazards, the driver must immediately place warning signs behind the tractor or trailer. "[T]he driver shall, as soon as possible, but in any event within 10 minutes, place the warning devices....in the following manner...."[403] The statute then requires three warning signs be placed as follows: (1) "[o]ne on the traffic side of and 4 paces ...from the stopped commercial vehicle"; (2) "[o]ne at 40 paces (approximately 30 meters or 100 feet) from the stopped commercial motor vehicle in the center of the traffic lane or shoulder"; and, (3) "[o]ne at 40 paces (approximately 30 meters or 100 feet) from the stopped commercial motor vehicle in the center of the traffic lane or shoulder occupied by the commercial motor vehicle and in the direction away from approaching traffic."[404]

Additionally, there are specific rules when the commercial vehicle stops in particular areas. In business or residential districts, for example, "[t]he

[402] 49 C.F.R. § 392.22(a).
[403] 49 C.F.R. § 392.22(b).
[404] Id.

placement of warning devices is not required…except…when street or highway lighting is insufficient to make commercial motor vehicle clearly discernable at a distance of 500 feet to persons on the highway."[405] If there is a hill, curve, or obstruction, then the rules require placement so as to notify drivers approaching this obstruction.

> *If a commercial motor vehicle is stopped within 500 feet of a curve, crest of a hill, or other obstruction to view, the driver shall place the warning signal required by paragraph (b)(1) of this section in the direction of the obstruction to view a distance of 100 feet to 500 feet from the stopped commercial motor vehicle so as to afford ample warning to other users of the highway.*[406]

When there is a "divided or one-way highway," then the warning signs must be placed at a distance of 200 feet, 100 feet, and 10 feet of the commercial vehicle.[407]

A driver or motor carrier who fails to follow these procedures may face liability for causing a third-party collision with the stopped vehicle.

5.5.1 Weather Hazards

Extreme weather and hazardous road conditions can give rise to accidents that subject the driver and motor carrier to liability. Truck companies commonly assert "Act-of-God" defenses in these situations. There is, however, a heightened responsibility of a professional driver to drive cautiously in light of the extreme conditions presented.

49 C.F.R. § 392.14 establishes standards for operation of the motor vehicle during hazardous conditions[408] stating that, "extreme caution in the operation of a commercial motor vehicle" is required when there are

---

[405] Id. at (b)(2)(iii).
[406] Id. at (b)(2)(iv).
[407] Id. at (b)(2)(v).
[408] 49 C.F.R. § 392.14.

hazardous conditions due to "snow, ice, sleet, fog, mist, rain, dust, or smoke, [which] adversely affect visibility or traction."[409] Further, "[s]peed shall be reduced when such conditions exist."[410]

When conditions become so extreme that safe operation is not possible, further operations by the commercial driver must be halted "and shall not be resumed until the commercial motor vehicle can be safely operated."[411] This does not mean that the commercial driver stops immediately. But, instead, "the commercial motor vehicle may be operated to the nearest point at which the safety of passengers is assured."[412]

Violation of these requirements may lead to liability despite the assertion of an "Act-of-God" defense related to weather conditions.

5.6 Driver Error Imputed to the Motor Carrier – *Respondeat Superior*

When the commercial driver commits an error within the course and scope of their employment, it often may be imputed to the motor carrier.[413] This is the basis of many commercial motor vehicle claims. However, that is often not the end of the line for most experienced truck accident lawyers.

Respondeat superior is a Latin term meaning "let the master answer."[414] This is a common law principle subjecting an employer to liability for the tortious actions of their employees when committed within the scope of their employment.[415] This doctrine's primary rationale is to assign responsibility to the party who has the authority and ability to control

---

[409] Id.
[410] Id.
[411] Id.
[412] Id.
[413] O.C.G.A. § 51-2-2.
[414] Endurance Am. Ins. Co. v. Cheyenne Partners, LLC, No. 20-0571, 2023 U.S. Dist. LEXIS 40244 at *13 (La. W.D., Mar. 9, 2023).
[415] Id.

the actions of the negligent actor. It also increases the likelihood that resources exist to compensate the injured parties.

To successfully impute a truck driver's negligence to the motor carrier under the doctrine of *respondeat superior*, the following elements must be established:

1. *Employment relationship:* First and foremost, it must be demonstrated that an employer-employee relationship existed between the truck driver and the motor carrier at the time of the accident.

2. *Scope of employment:* The negligent act must have occurred within the scope of the truck driver's employment. This generally means that the driver was performing tasks on behalf of the motor carrier, acting within the time and space limits of their job, and furthering the interests of the employer.

3. *Negligent act:* The truck driver's conduct must be negligent, which means a failure to exercise reasonable care under the circumstances. This may include actions such as speeding, failing to obey traffic signals, or driving under the influence, among others.[416]

Like any other tort case, a careful examination of the employment and agency relationship of the driver is important.

5.7 Improper Dispatch by Motor Carrier

Motor carriers dispatch drivers on transportation assignments or jobs. Dispatch generally refers to the route assigned, load provided, and permission granted to travel. Dispatch arguably imputes upon the motor carrier a duty to ensure that the driver is complying with their responsibilities.

---

[416] See, e.g., <u>Broadnax v. Daniel Custom Constr., LLC</u>, 315 Ga. App. 291 (2012).

Specifically, the FMCSR prohibit the motor carrier from encouraging its employees to violate the regulations. "No person shall aid, abet, encourage, or require a motor carrier or its employees to violate the rules of this chapter."[417] An example might be a situation in which a motor carrier encourages or otherwise assists a professional driver to violate their hours-of-service limitations.

Recall, the hours-of-service rules expressly require the motor carrier to <u>not</u> permit the driver to operate a vehicle if they are over hours or will be over hours.[418] This applies to both property carrying and passenger carrying vehicles.

The motor carrier also cannot dispatch a load knowing that the driver must exceed speed limits to complete the delivery in the expected timeframe. Specifically, "[n]o motor carrier shall schedule a run nor permit nor require the operation of any commercial motor vehicle between points in such period of time as would necessitate the commercial motor vehicle being operated at speeds greater than those prescribed by the jurisdictions in or through which the commercial motor vehicle is being operated."[419]

These rules and others, including those related to maintenance (discussed above), establish certain requirements for the motor carrier to ensure the rules are followed at the times of dispatch.

5.8 Negligent Hiring, Retention, and Entrustment

Earlier in this Manual, we outlined the requirements of the FMCSR for a motor carrier when hiring, investigating, retaining, and entrusting drivers. When a motor carrier fails to properly investigate their drivers pursuant to Federal law and this causes an accident, there may be a claim for negligent hiring, retention, and entrustment.

---

[417] 49 C.F.R. § 390.13.
[418] 49 C.F.R. § 395.3(b); 49 C.F.R. § 395.5(b).
[419] 49 C.F.R. § 392.6.

The FMCSR make clear that a motor carrier must investigate its prospective drivers.[420] This investigation includes an employment inquiry made to prior, DOT-covered employers.[421] Specifically, the motor carrier must inquire into the driver's health and obtain a valid medical examiner's certificate.[422] The motor carrier must also investigate the driver's "motor vehicle record" for all locations of the driver's CDL or prior CDLs within the preceding 3 years.[423]

The investigative inquiry continues after the driver is hired. It includes an annual inquiry into the driver's records.[424] These (and other duties imposed by Federal regulations) can form the basis of a negligent hiring, supervision, and entrustment claim against the motor carrier. This type of claim will be based on state law and informed by the Federal standards.

In Georgia, the state Supreme Court has held that "a defendant employer has a duty to exercise ordinary care not to hire or retain an employee the employer knew or should have known posed a risk of harm to others where it is reasonably foreseeable from the employee's 'tendencies' or propensities that the employee could cause the type of harm sustained by the plaintiff."[425] Because the Federal standards impose investigation and supervision requirements on motor carriers for commercial drivers, a failure to abide by these standards in conjunction with state-law tort claims can form the basis of a cause of action.

"[T]he motor carrier industry's needs and concerns involving drivers extend to a range of past accidents, incidents, mishaps, occurrences and events well beyond those encompassed by § 390.5."[426] Therefore, investigation into these instances (and failure to do so) is key to a negligence claim for hiring, retention, supervision, and entrustment.

---

[420] 49 C.F.R. § 391.23.
[421] 49 C.F.R. § 391.23 (c)(2).
[422] 49 C.F.R. § 391.23(m).
[423] 49 C.F.R. § 391.23(a)(1).
[424] 49 C.F.R. § 391.25.
[425] Munroe v. Universal Health Services, Inc., 277 Ga. 861, 862 (2004).
[426] Cassara v. DAC Services, Inc., 276 F.3d 1210, 1225 (10th Cir. 2002).

5.9 Improper Loading and Inspection of Load

In prior sections, we discussed the requirements of the FMCSR for the proper loading and inspection of loads. Failure to comply with these requirements can form the basis for the motor carrier's liability.

The Federal Regulations governing cargo and loading establish standards for the inspection of cargo and loading before operation of the motor vehicle.

"A driver may not operate a commercial motor vehicle and a motor carrier may not require or permit a driver to operate a commercial motor vehicle unless:" (1) "the commercial motor vehicle's cargo is properly distributed and adequately secured..."; (2) "The commercial motor vehicle's tailgate, tailboard, doors, tarpaulins, spare tire and other equipment used in its operation, and the means of fastening the commercial motor vehicle's cargo, are secured"; and (3) "The commercial motor vehicle's cargo or any other object does not" obstruct the driver's view or prevent the driver's movement.[427]

The driver is required to "assure himself/herself" that the cargo is secure and weight properly distributed.[428] Therefore, the driver also has an active role in ensuring that the cargo does not contribute to an accident.

> **Pro Note:** Even though the law recently changed to eliminate pre-trip inspections of the vehicle, the law remains that the driver must assure himself that the cargo is properly secured before driving.

In the event a load contributes to an accident or the severity of damages suffered, a competent attorney will examine whether the inspection requirements were followed.

---

[427] 49 C.F.R. § 392.9.
[428] 49 C.F.R. § 392.9(b).

6

LITIGATION ISSUES IN COMMERCIAL MOTOR VEHICLE CASES

There are unique litigation issues in commercial motor vehicle cases. This section will cover the following: (1) Overview of Commercial Motor Vehicle Litigation; (2) Pre-Suit Investigation into Commercial Motor Vehicle Cases; (3) Discovery in Commercial Motor Vehicle Litigation; and (4) Expert Issues in Commercial Motor Vehicle Cases. This Manual will not discuss the basics of personal injury cases but will, instead, focus on the unique issues in commercial motor vehicle cases.

6.1 Overview of Commercial Motor Vehicle Litigation

In our firm, we run on systems and forms. A good system, created once, delivers dividends for every case of that type going forward. For truck accident cases, we have a series of checklists for the various parts of the cases. Below is our Master Checklist. The sections that follow will discuss in detail certain key elements of the same.

6.1.1 Master Checklist

Below is a general checklist for the handling of a commercial vehicle collision on the Plaintiff's side. Each case is different, and the tasks/issues listed may not apply in every case.

Investigation:

- ☐ Preservation Letter:
    - ___ Commercial Driver
    - ___ Commercial Carrier
    - ___ Insurer

- ☐ FOIA Request:
    - ___ Main Office
    - ___ Regional Office
    - ___ State Office

- ☐ Open Records Request:
    - ___ Police
    - ___ 911
    - ___ Specialized Investigation Unit

- ☐ Scene Investigation:
    - ___ Consider reconstructionist
    - ___ Local investigation for witnesses and video
    - ___ Markers for incident

- ☐ Incident Investigation:
    - ___ Private investigation
    - ___ Social investigation
    - ___ Prior incident investigation

- ☐ Vehicle Investigation:
    - ___ Thorough inspection of commercial vehicle
    - ___ Thorough inspection of private vehicle
    - ___ Download of data from engine control module

    __ 3-D rendering of incident

    __ Follow up on preservation request

☐ Reconstruction:

    __ Speed calculation

    __ Distance calculation

    __ Timing determination

    __ Consider human factors issues

☐ Medical:

    __ Marshall all medical records

    __ Review medical records in detail

    __ Summarize medical records

    __ Consider medical expert for injuries

    __ Consider billing expert

    __ Consider lifecare plan

☐ Witness:

    __ Contact witnesses

    __ Private Investigator

    __ Interview witnesses

    __ Prepare affidavits or recorded statements

    __ Consult with reconstructionist on witness statements and data

☐ Legal:

    __ Research Federal standards

    __ Research state standards

    __ Review industry standards

    __ Consider expert review

Pre-Suit Issues:

☐ Damages:

    __ Gather all relevant records

    __ Consider statements of character/life witnesses

    __ Prepare life care plan if applicable
    __ Open estate if applicable
    __ Appoint administrator if applicable
    __ Consider Day in the Life Video
    __ Review journal entries of client
    __ Verdict research

☐ Demand:
    __ Review investigative work
    __ Review inspection reports
    __ Consider expert statement
    __ Consider reconstruction issues
    __ Review Federal, state, and industry standards
    __ Determine settlement value through analysis

Litigation:

☐ Pleadings:
    __ Draft Complaint
    __ Research entities involved
    __ Consider claims against employer, broker, owner, operator, insurer, shipper
    __ Consider claims against commercial driver
    __ Consider types of causes of action
    __ Review Federal, state, and industry standards

☐ Discovery:
    __ Prepare written discovery to employer, broker, owner, operator, insurer, shipper
    __ Prepare written discovery to commercial driver
    __ Prepare discovery to third-parties (medical providers, governmental authorities, prior employers, other relevant third parties)
    __ Take depositions of witnesses depending on the case: plaintiff, commercial driver, manager/supervisor, safety

personnel, investigating officer, specialized investigator, accident reconstructionist plaintiff/defense, human factors plaintiff/defense, industry expert plaintiff/defense, character witnesses, prior employers, prior medical providers, etc.

☐ Pre-Trial Motions:
__ Daubert motions on all experts
__ Motions to Compel on any issues
__ Standard pre-trial motions

☐ Trial:
__ PTO
__ Determine evidence to be admitted
__ Exhibit Notebook
__ Affidavits for Admission
__ Pre-Trial Depositions
__ *Voir Dire*
__ Opening
__ Examinations
__ Trial Motions
__ Closing

The most important thing to remember when handling a case against a motor carrier is that it is a professional company, federally regulated, with numerous responsibilities. Everything you do should emphasize this point.

6.2 Pre-Suit Investigation

A truck accident case requires deep investigation at the beginning of the claim. Immediate attention is key, as significant evidence evaporates quickly. Let's look at the steps that our office takes.

6.2.1 Preservation Letter

When initially signing onto a commercial motor vehicle case, the first step is to send a "preservation letter" or "preservation demand." This is a formal letter that notifies the potential defendants you have a claim against them and plan to file an action. The letter specifically identifies the types of documents and other items the defendant is expected or required to keep. It is important to note that a motor carrier is <u>not</u> required to maintain documents unless it has received notice of a claim.

To be sure all relevant evidence is preserved for our clients, we take the following steps:

* identify the potential defendant(s),

* identify the potentially relevant items they may possess and must preserve, and

* send a <u>certified</u> letter to the defendant(s) stating that our client plans to file suit.

Once the letter is received, Georgia law requires the relevant items be preserved.[429]

> **Pro Note:** Send the preservation letter via certified mail, so you can later prove that it was received.

Under the rules of civil procedure, if the item is not preserved and the circumstances warrant it, the court can sanction (or punish) the motor carrier for failing to maintain the evidence. These punishments can even include striking of the answer, if the actions are egregious.[430]

---

[429] <u>Creek House Seafood & Grill, LLC v. Provatas</u>, 358 Ga. App. 727 (2021).
[430] <u>Id.</u>

In our opinion, the preservation letter should be limited to the items you really believe need be preserved. Some attorneys throw in everything except the kitchen sink. However, these kitchen-sink preservation requests are often unreasonable and difficult to enforce in court.

6.2.2 Example Preservation Letter

Here is an example of a preservation letter and the type of items a truck accident attorney may request. Whether each of these items is relevant will depend on your case.

INSERT DATE

<u>Via Certified Mail</u>

INSERT DEFENDANTS NAME

> **Date of Automobile Collision:** *INSERT DETAILS*
> **Our Client:** *INSERT DETAILS*
> **Accident Report No.:** *INSERT DETAILS*
> **Location:** *INSERT DETAILS*

Dear Sir/Madam:

This letter is written to *INSERT DEFENDANTS NAME* ("*INSERT*" or "you"). We represent *INSERT CLAIMANT'S NAME* ("*INSERT*") who was injured in the above-referenced automobile collision (the "Incident") for which you are wholly responsible.

Although you should already know that potential claims may result from the Incident, you are hereby placed on formal notice of potential claims regarding the above-referenced matter. These potential claims include, but are not limited to, claims related to personal injury, pain and suffering, and any and all claims which may be related to the above-referenced incident.

It is hereby demanded, pursuant to *Georgia law*, that you preserve any and all items, pictures, videos, receipts, documents, records, related in any way to the incident. *Georgia law* requires that you preserve any relevant evidence, and your failure to do so will result in sanctions against you. <u>*Baxley v. Hakiel Indus.*</u>, *282 Ga. 312 (2007)*. *"Spoliation refers to the destruction or failure to preserve evidence that is necessary to contemplated or pending litigation. Such conduct creates the presumption that the evidence would have been harmful to the spoliator."* <u>Id.</u> (internal citations omitted). These sanctions can include, but are not limited to, striking of the answer.

This preservation request specifically includes but is not limited to the following items:

1. Any and all videos and recordings relating to the incident;

2. Any and all photographs relating to the incident;

3. The tractor-trailer, in its unaltered condition, being operated by your driver ("Your Driver");

4. The title and registration for the tractor-trailer being driven by Your Driver at the time of the incident;

5. Any and all procedures, manuals, and protocols related in any way to operation of the tractor-trailer;

6. Any and all training materials for Your Driver;

7. The recordings, CAD-reports, police reports, accident reports or witness statements;

8. Any and all documents reflecting communications, including but not limited to text messages, voicemails, and/or cell phone records relating to the incident and any investigation thereof;

9. Your Driver's complete driver's qualification file, pursuant to 49 C.F.R. 391.51;

10. Your Driver's post-accident drug and alcohol testing results;

11. Any lease contracts or agreements covering Your Driver or the tractor-trailer at issue;

12. Any data or print-out from an on-board recording device or GPS system for the tractor-trailer Your Driver was operating for the day of the incident;

13. Post-accident maintenance and repair records regarding the tractor-trailer Your Driver was operating;

14. Six months of pre-accident maintenance and repair records regarding the tractor-trailer Your Driver was operating;

15. The daily inspection report for the tractor-trailer Your Driver was operating for the day of the incident and the one week prior, 49 C.F.R. 396.11 and 396.13;

16. Your driver's daily logs for the involved driver for the day of the incident and the 30 days prior, 49 C.F.R. Part 395;

17. Any documents relating to the weight of the tractor-trailer Your Driver was operating at the time of the incident, including oversized permits or weight tickets; and,

18. Any and all other documents which may be related in any way to the above-referenced claims.

Please forward this communication to your insurance carrier immediately.

Very Truly Yours,

Insert Signature

6.2.3 FOIA Request

Another early step is a Freedom of Information Act ("FOIA") request. The Freedom of Information Act permits interested persons to obtain documents from certain Federal agencies, including the Department of Transportation. The request may produce information not found in SAFER, SMS, and MCMIS.

6.2.4 Example FOIA Request

Below is an example FOIA request. A FOIA request should be sent immediately upon receipt of the case. It should be tailored to fit the facts and circumstances of the case and the law in your state. Some of the items requested below will not be beneficial in some cases. In other cases, there may be additional crucial information that is not listed as it arises only in that specific instance. A well-drafted FOIA request is essential to setting the case on the right path. We often send FOIA requests to the main office, regional service center, and state office. Items in italics below are replaced.

INSERT DATE

<u>Via Certified Mail</u>

Federal Motor Carrier Safety Administration
Attn: FOIA Team MC-MMI
Insert Address

FOIA REQUEST

Federal Motor Carrier: *INSERT DETAILS*
Federal Motor Carrier No.: *INSERT DETAILS*
Commercial Driver: *INSERT DETAILS*
Commercial Vehicle: *INSERT DETAILS*

Date of Incident: *INSERT DETAILS*
Location of Incident: *INSERT DETAILS*
Our Client: *INSERT DETAILS*

Dear Sir/Madam:

This letter is written to you as an officer for the above-referenced governmental agency. We represent *INSERT CLAIMANT'S NAME* ("*INSERT*") who was injured in the above-referenced collision (the "Incident") with the above referenced Motor Carrier.

We request the following information under the Freedom of Information Act: (1) documents regarding regulatory fines for the Motor Carrier for the prior 10 years; (2) documents showing agency intervention, compliance reviews, and safety ratings for the Motor Carrier for the prior 10 years; (3) documents regarding inspection reports for the Commercial Driver and Commercial Vehicle for the prior 10 years; (4) the Form OP-1 for the Motor Carrier; (5) the Form MCS-150; (6) any other documents or reports regarding motor vehicle accidents, injuries, and investigations for the Motor Carrier, the Commercial Driver, and the Commercial Vehicle in the prior 10 years; and (7) any publicly available information in your possession regarding the Commercial Driver or the Motor Carrier as it relates to their compliance with the FMCSR, injuries, accidents, violations, inspections, or fitness.

We will pay any charges required up to *$250.00*. If charges are in excess of *$250.00*, please contact our firm for additional authorization. My fax, telephone number, and email are listed below. Please contact me if you need any additional information.

Very Truly Yours,

Insert Signature

6.2.5 Open Records Request

The next step is to send an "open records request" to the appropriate state and local agencies. In Georgia, this request is made pursuant to the Georgia Open Records Act.[431] It follows the same type of request that we send to Federal agencies.

6.2.6 Example Open Records Request

Below is an example Open Records Request. An open records request should be sent immediately upon receipt of the case. It should be tailored to fit the facts and circumstances of the case and the law in your state. Some of the items requested below will not be beneficial in some cases. In other cases, there may be additional crucial information that is not listed as it arises only in that specific instance. A well-drafted Open Records Request is essential to setting the case on the right path. Items in italics below are replaced.

INSERT DATE

Via Certified Mail

Georgia Dep't of Public Safety
Motor Carrier Compliance Division
Attn: OPEN RECORDS REQUEST
Insert

OPEN RECORDS REQUEST

Federal Motor Carrier: *INSERT DETAILS*
Federal Motor Carrier No.: *INSERT DETAILS*
Commercial Driver: *INSERT DETAILS*
Commercial Vehicle: *INSERT DETAILS*

---

[431] O.C.G.A. § 50-18-72(a) *et seq.*

Date of Incident: *INSERT DETAILS*
Location of Incident: *INSERT DETAILS*
Our Client: *INSERT DETAILS*

Dear Sir/Madam:

This letter is written to you as an officer for the above-referenced governmental agency. We represent *INSERT CLAIMANT'S NAME* (*"INSERT"*) who was injured in the above-referenced collision (the "Incident") with the above referenced Motor Carrier.

We are writing pursuant to the Opens Records Act, O.C.G.A. § 50-18-72(a) *et seq.* Pursuant to the Open Records Act, we request the following information: (1) documents regarding regulatory fines for the Motor Carrier for the prior 10 years; (2) documents showing agency intervention, compliance reviews, and safety ratings for the Motor Carrier for the prior 10 years; (3) documents regarding inspection reports for the Commercial Driver and Commercial Vehicle for the prior 10 years; (4) the Form OP-1 for the Motor Carrier; (5) the Form MCS-150; (6) any other documents or reports regarding motor vehicle accidents, injuries, and investigations for the Motor Carrier, the Commercial Driver, and the Commercial Vehicle in the prior 10 years; and (7) any publicly available information in your possession regarding the Commercial Driver or the Motor Carrier as it relates to their compliance with the FMCSR or Georgia law, injuries, accidents, violations, inspections, or fitness.

We will pay any charges required up to *$250.00*. If charges are in excess of *$250.00*, please contact our firm for <u>additional</u> authorization. My fax, telephone number, and email are listed below. Please contact me if you need any additional information.

Very Truly Yours,

Insert Signature

6.3 Investigation of Scene, Incident, and Vehicles

As is in any significant personal injury case, the investigation of the scene, incident, and vehicles are key elements to explore in preparing the case. This section will discuss the potential importance of expert assistance in investigating each of these issues.

When investigating a commercial motor vehicle case, if necessary, we engage an accident reconstruction expert to investigate the scene. We also personally visit the scene to collect evidence. You will be surprised by how helpful this action can be in preparing your case. Here are some of the items for which we are looking at the time:

- **Vehicles** – You will want to inspect and obtain or document all physical evidence possible from the damaged vehicles, including third-party vehicles damaged in the accident. Make certain to note the tire wear, brake conditions, lighting systems and any other physical evidence that could demonstrate damage or relate to the cause of the accident. It is also important to personally download all of the electronic data recorded in the truck. Downloads may reveal speed, acceleration, braking, equipment malfunction and more.

- **Lighting Conditions and Weather** - The weather conditions and time of day may affect the accident. Take any steps possible to record the conditions at the time of the collision. The use of camera footage (such as from dash cameras or security footage) and weather reports are two good methods. Recreating the truck accident as closely as possible is an essential element of a commercial motor vehicle case.

- **Road Conditions** - Road conditions may also affect the standard of care expected of motorists. For example, roads that are wet, poorly maintained, or covered with gravel or debris may contribute to the incident and trigger a heightened duty of care.

Also, skid marks on the road are a strong indicator of when the driver began hard braking. The length of the skid marks may indicate the distance that the driver travelled once applying the brakes. This length will be affected by vehicle weight and velocity (speed) of travel. Again, this is an important topic to discuss with the crash reconstruction expert.

- **Remains and Debris** - Debris from the scene can also assist in accident reconstruction. Specifically, it helps determine the points of collision between the vehicles. We recommend creating an area diagram demonstrating where and how far debris from the accident is scattered.

When there is an injury justifying the expense, scene, incident, and vehicle investigations are absolutely critical in a commercial motor vehicle case. Truck companies are well-funded and will, almost certainly, have experts on the scene immediately following the accident, if the claim appears to present significant exposure. Therefore, the plaintiff's attorney must go to these same ends (or further) to collect evidence. Key information, such as accident debris, paint markings (from government investigation), and videos may go missing without prompt attention.

6.4 Accident Reconstruction

An accident reconstructionist is an expert who investigates all relevant factors and recreates the accident. In general, accident reconstructionists fall into two camps: (a) engineers; and (b) former police officers.[432] An engineer generally has traditional education in the field of recreating accidents. A former police officer receives training through their time as a civil servant.

---

[432] National Society of Professional Engineers, Website, https://www.nspe.org/resources/issues-and-advocacy/professional-policies-and-position-statements/accident-reconstruction (last accessed Apr. 28, 2023).

An accident reconstructionist applies their specialized knowledge of law enforcement procedures and experience investigating traffic accidents to determine the cause of an accident. They identify exactly how the physical collision occurred, analyze the evidence, and recreate the circumstances surrounding the accident in question. This may involve a thorough investigation of the accident scene, interviews with witnesses, and a review of any available police reports or other relevant documentation. They take data points from these measurements and recreate the accident as best as possible.[433]

In prior cases, we've employed an accident reconstructionist to recreate (or model) the collision and demonstrate the exact viewpoint of a commercial vehicle driver.

This includes determining the exact speed of vehicles at each point in time as the accident was playing out.

Other types of expert witnesses or consultants and their roles in the development of a case are discussed further in this Manual.

---

[433] Atlanta Engineering Services, Inc., Website, https://www.atlantaeng.com/accidentreconstruction.html (last visited Apr. 28, 2023).

6.5 Discovery in Commercial Motor Vehicle Cases

Discovery in a commercial motor vehicle case utilizes the same tools as other civil claims. This includes interrogatories, requests for production, requests for admissions, third-party requests for production, and depositions.[434] Each of these will be discussed in turn below.

6.5.1 Interrogatories

The Plaintiff's interrogatories listed below will generally follow the local rules of civil procedure and focus on the requirements of the Federal regulations. In general, this means licensing[435], hiring and training,[436] hours of service,[437] drug/alcohol testing,[438] and inspection/maintenance of the tractor-trailer.[439] Some of these regulations may not fit your case. There are additional regulations that may apply.

Here are some of the truck-specific interrogatories that we utilize on a case-by-case basis:

* Please describe your relationship with TRUCK DRIVER ("TRUCK DRIVER") on the day of the Incident, including whether at the time of the Incident he was acting as your agent, furthering your business, or acting as your employee.

* If you are now or have ever been a party to any litigation (other than this civil action) for claims involving TRUCK DRIVER, speeding, or driving too fast for conditions, please list the title of each such action, including the names of all parties; the court

---

[434] O.C.G.A. § 9-11-30, 34, & 36.
[435] 49 C.F.R. § 383.
[436] 49 C.F.R. § 391.
[437] 49 C.F.R. § 395.
[438] 49 C.F.R. § 382.
[439] 49 C.F.R. § 396.

in which it was brought; its civil action number; and whether you were deposed in that case and, if so, the name, address, and phone number of the individual(s) who have a copy of said deposition.

- Please list any and all citations, warning, and/or traffic tickets that TRUCK DRIVER received in the last 10 years, including in your description the date it was received, the offense it was received for, and the names and addresses of the parties involved.

- Please explain in detail any and all efforts made by you prior to hiring Defendant TRUCK DRIVER to determine if he was a competent and capable operator of a tractor-trailer.

- Please state your company policies for investigating the driving capabilities of potential or current drivers, including (a) the policy for background checks; (b) the policy for investigating motor vehicle infractions/accidents of the driver; (c) the policy for drug/alcohol detection; and (d) the policy for determining if a driver is sleep deprived. For any such policy, please state if the Policy was oral or written.

- Are you aware of any other motor vehicle accident involving Defendant TRUCK DRIVER? If your answer is anything other than an unqualified "no," please describe the motor vehicle accident including (a) the parties involved and their contact information; (b) the location of the accident; (c) the date of the accident; and, (d) how you came to know of the accident.

- Did Defendant TRUCK DRIVER suffer from any physical ailments or disabilities whatsoever related in any way to his ability to operate a vehicle (including but not limited to disorders related to sleep, wakefulness, concentration etc.) at the time of the Incident? If your answer is anything other than an unqualified "no," please state (a) the diagnosis; (b) the contact information for the doctors involved in treatment of Defendant TRUCK DRIVER; and (c) when and how you became aware of the ailment/disability.

- Please state any intoxicating beverages, drugs, or medicines (prescription or otherwise) of any kind that Defendant TRUCK DRIVER took within the twenty-four (24) hours preceding the Incident.

- Please state whether or not, as of the date of the Incident, the tractor trailer driven by Defendant TRUCK DRIVER had any mechanical defects and, if so, the nature of the same.

- Please state where Defendant TRUCK DRIVER had been immediately prior to the Incident and where he was traveling at the time of the collision.

- Please describe in detail the load that Defendant TRUCK DRIVER was hauling at the time of the incident including (a) the materials in the load; (b) the approximate weight of the load; and (c) whether the load had been checked to determine it was not overweight.

- Did you require drivers, such as Mr. TRUCK DRIVER, to record daily driver logs? If so, please state (a) whether the logs are electronic, manual, or both; (b) whether Mr. TRUCK DRIVER filled out a log for the day of the Incident and the 1 month prior to the Incident; (c) whether you still have the logs for Mr. TRUCK DRIVER; and (d) whether you keep a record of any driver log violations for Mr. TRUCK DRIVER.

- If you no longer have the driver logs for Mr. TRUCK DRIVER for the day of the Incident and 1 month prior to the Incident, please state (a) what happened to the logs; (b) if the logs were destroyed and the date the logs were destroyed; and, (c) the name, address, and telephone number of all persons involved in the destruction of the logs.

- Did you require drivers, such as Mr. TRUCK DRIVER, to perform daily inspections of the tractor and trailer they were operating? If so, please state (a) whether the inspection reports are electronic, manual, or both; (b) whether Mr. TRUCK DRIVER filled out an inspection report for the day of the Incident and the 1 month prior to the Incident; and (c) whether you still have the inspection report for Mr. TRUCK DRIVER.

- If you no longer have the inspection reports for Mr. TRUCK DRIVER for the day of the Incident and 1 month prior to the Incident, please state (a) what happened to the inspection reports; (b) if the inspection reports were destroyed; (c) the date the inspection reports were destroyed; and, (d) the name, address, and telephone number of all persons involved in the destruction of the inspection reports.

- Please state whether or not you required Defendant TRUCK DRIVER to submit to a post collision drug and alcohol test and, if so, please identify the name, location, time, and date of the drug and alcohol test.

- Please state whether you have retained a driver qualification file for Defendant TRUCK DRIVER and, if so, please list the documents in that file.

- Please state the method by which compensation was determined for the payment of Defendant TRUCK DRIVER for the trip during which the Incident occurred.

- Does your truck contain an on-board computer, GPS, black box, or other electronic control module? If your answer is anything other than an unqualified "no," please state (a) the type of machine it contains; (b) whether or not any electronic data was recorded as to this Incident; (c) if the data no longer exists, why the data has been destroyed and when it occurred; and (d) if the data still exists, the name, address, and telephone number of persons storing the data.

* Please list any and all manuals, driving standards, and/or instructions you provide to your drivers.

* If you contend that Defendant TRUCK DRIVER was not acting under your direction and control at the time of the Incident, please state the name, address, and telephone number of who you contend Defendant TRUCK DRIVER was working for at the time of the Incident.

6.5.2 Requests for Production

In general, requests for production will focus on documents related to the accident, the vehicle, and the driver. In general, these include the following: (a) daily inspection reports; (b) maintenance records; (c) hours of service records; (d) speed, engine, and GPS information; and, (e) driver qualifications, etc. There are additional rules that may apply.

Here are some of the truck-specific requests for production that we utilize on a case-by-case basis:

* Please produce any and all traffic citations that Mr. TRUCK DRIVER has received in the last 10 years.

* Please produce the results of all investigations into Mr. TRUCK DRIVER's driving history including any Motor Vehicle Reports, citations, accidents, or license suspensions.

- Please permit the Plaintiff to inspect the tractor-trailer, in its unaltered condition, being operated by TRUCK DRIVER on the day of the Incident.

- Any and all training materials provided to TRUCK DRIVER.

- Mr. TRUCK DRIVER's complete driver's qualification file, pursuant to 49 C.F.R. 391.51.

- Mr. TRUCK DRIVER's complete personnel file.

- Mr. TRUCK DRIVER's post-accident drug and alcohol testing results.

- All lease contracts or agreements covering Mr. TRUCK DRIVER or the tractor-trailer at issue.

- All data or print-out from an on-board recording device, black box, electronic control module, or GPS system for the tractor-trailer for the day of the incident.

- All post-Incident maintenance and repair records regarding the tractor and trailer.

- All maintenance and repair records for the tractor and trailer for the 6 months prior to the Incident.

- Please provide the daily inspection report for the tractor trailer for the day of the Incident and the 1 week prior, 49 C.F.R. 396.11 and 396.13

- Please provide the driver's daily logs for Mr. TRUCK DRIVER for the day of the Incident and the 30 days prior, 49 C.F.R. Part 395

- Please provide any documents showing the hours of service Mr. TRUCK DRIVER worked the day of the Incident and the 30 days prior.

- Any documents that would relate to the weight of the tractor-trailer at the time of the incident, including oversized permits or weight tickets

- Any human resources or discipline documents for Mr. TRUCK DRIVER related to driving, sleepiness, speeding, hours of service violations, or auto accidents.

- The preventability assessment performed by the Company for the Incident.

- All medical reports, medical tests, alcohol tests, or drug tests for Mr. TRUCK DRIVER.

- The route manifest for Mr. TRUCK DRIVER for the day of the Incident and the trip in question.

- Any reports of audits of Mr. TRUCK DRIVER's driver logs for the day of the Incident and the 30 days prior to the Incident.

- Any documents showing the type of load being hauled and the weight of load being hauled.

- The payroll records for Mr. TRUCK DRIVER for the day of the Incident and the 30 days prior to the Incident.

6.5.3 Requests for Admissions

Some attorneys send detailed requests for admission on facts that are obviously in dispute. At our firm, we use them more for authentication of evidence and for stipulation of undisputed issues of fact.

> **Pro Note:** As a practice point, only send RFAs on issues that are clearly undisputed and are necessary elements in proving the case.

6.5.4 Third-Party Requests for Production

In our firm, we send requests to produce to many types of third parties, including employers, medical providers, and health insurers. Evidence acquired from these parties is most useful in testing the accuracy of the motor carrier and the truck driver's statements in their employment application, during medical examinations, and post-accident. Recall, the FMCSR require the application, for example, to be sworn as true and correct.[440] Third-party requests can be an excellent way to find inaccuracies and challenge the credibility of the commercial driver and commercial carrier.

6.5.5 Depositions

The deposition is an extremely powerful tool in a truck crash case. In general, the need for and sequence of depositions will be as follows: (i) Plaintiff; (ii) Driver; (iii) Witness(es); (iv) Police Officer(s); (v) Motor Carrier Representative; (vi) Shipper; (vii) Broker; (viii) Maintenance Company; (ix) Intermodal Company; (x) Parent Company; (xi) Defense Expert(s) (such as an Accident Reconstructionist); and, (xii) Medical Expert(s). The depositions taken will depend on the facts and circumstances of the case, including the theory of liability and potential recovery at trial.

In a serious commercial motor vehicle case, the most important depositions (in our experience) are the commercial driver and the commercial representative. Under Georgia (and Federal) law, a 30(b)(6) deposition allows a party to name a corporation or other entity as the deponent and requires the corporation to designate one or more

---

[440] 49 C.F.R. § 391.21(b)(12).

individuals to testify on its behalf regarding the matters set forth in the deposition notice.[441]

The designated individuals must be knowledgeable about the designated topics and must speak on behalf of the corporation (rather than on their own behalf). The notice must describe the topics to be addressed with reasonable particularity to allow the corporation to determine which of its employees is best suited to speak on its behalf.

During the deposition, the designated individuals must testify about the designated topics to the best of their knowledge and information. They may be questioned about the corporation's relevant policies, procedures, and practices. The corporation is obligated to make a good-faith effort to prepare its designated representative(s) for the deposition, and the representative(s) must testify to matters known or "reasonably available" to the corporation.[442]

Thanks to the significant number of requirements on motor carriers, a 30(b)(6) deposition can be the best method for determining the motor carrier's compliance with the rules. Inquiry into their methods for compliance is key.

6.6 Expert Issues in Commercial Motor Vehicle Cases

At this point, it should be apparent that handling a commercial motor vehicle case requires a detailed, technical understanding of many facets of the situation. You will depend heavily upon the information derived from police reports, government safety investigations, medical records, and company records. Even an experienced truck attorney will routinely utilize the services of experts. Very often, the expertise of third parties is indispensable in understanding and developing a case, when

---

[441] Fed. R. Civ. P. 30(b)(6); O.C.G.A. § 9-11-30(b)(6).
[442] Id.

the potential recovery justifies the expense. The experts you may need include:

- *Accident Reconstructionist:* We cannot adequately state the importance of hiring a trained and competent accident reconstructionist. This expert recreates what happened at the time of the crash. They can develop visual depictions of the accident and provide exact measurements for relevant items, such as field of view, braking distance, speed at impact, maneuvers prior to impact, movement after impact, etc.[443]

- *Human Factors Expert:* A human factors expert can be critical when the accident involves issues of timing, perception, and response of the commercial driver involved in the collision. These experts study human reaction time and perception in stressful situations, such as motor vehicle collisions.[444]

- *Biomechanical Expert:* A biomechanical expert testifies on the physical forces present in an accident and how they affect the human body and the potential injuries inflicted. "[B]iomechanical engineers typically are found to be qualified to render an opinion as to the forces generated in a particular accident and the general types of injuries those forces may generate."[445]

- *Roadway Expert:* Design standard cases are, in essence, professional malpractice cases. A roadway expert's testimony will be necessary to prove that the road or construction did not substantially comply with engineering and design standards in effect at the time it was built.[446]

---

[443] Accident Reconstructionist Website, https://www.collisionspecialistsinc.com/ (last accessed Apr. 28, 2024).
[444] DOT v. Delor, 351 Ga. App. 414 (2019) (discussing human factors expert in automobile collision case).
[445] Bowers v. Norfolk Southern Corp, 537 F.Supp.2d 1343, 1377 (M.D.Ga. 2007).
[446] Steele v. Dept. of Transp., 271 Ga. App. 374 (2005).

- *Trucking Law, Policy & Procedures:* An expert will look at Federal law and the company's policies and procedures to render an opinion on the application of the standards to the facts of the case. This expert will likely be permitted to testify as to the Federal standards, as opposed to commonly known Rules of the Road.[447]

- *Mechanical/Maintenance Expert:* A mechanical expert examines the crashed vehicle for defects and to determine whether the vehicle is in working order. Further, s/he may be able to determine whether the vehicle's operational condition contributed to the accident or the damage suffered. The expert may also be able to compare the state of the equipment with the records of repair and maintenance to identify inconsistencies.[448]

- *Medical Experts:* A medical expert will be able to review the medical records of the victim to determine the extent of harm suffered. Further, the expert will be able to review any relevant medical records of the driver to determine whether a medical condition or medications potentially impaired the driver's performance.

Finding, reviewing, hiring, and working with experts is tricky. Experts are pricey, and many claim to the "best". However, there is a significant disparity in expert quality for truck collision cases. Please reach out to us if you need help with this process.

---

[447] <u>Castle-Foster v. Cintas Corp.</u>, 2021 US. Dist. LEXIS 28145 (S.D. Ga. Feb. 16, 2021).
[448] Accident Reconstructionist Website, https://www.collisionspecialistsinc.com/ (last accessed Apr. 28, 2024).

7

CONCLUSION

We wrote this Manual to provide you with a basic understanding of the complex legal issues in truck collision cases. It is our pleasure to provide you this help and support.

Please understand this Manual alone is insufficient to handle a case appropriately. It takes years of experience to master this nuanced area of tort law.

Should you find yourself involved in such a case, please consider reaching out to the Weatherby Law Firm. Please call my cell, 770-363-0354, or send me an email at alex@weatherbylawfirm.com. We are a group of hardworking, knowledgeable professionals with the ability to maximize your client's recovery in these types of cases.

Sincerely,

Alex Weatherby

Weatherby Law Firm. PC
750 Piedmont Avenue NE
Atlanta GA, 30308
alex@weatherbylawfirm.com
404-793-0026 (office)
404-793-0106 (fax)
770-363-0354 (cell)
www.weatherbylawfirm.com

Made in the USA
Columbia, SC
25 July 2024

39356599R00098